Radio Scriptwriting

Radio Scriptwriting

Edited by Sam Boardman-Jacobs

seren

Seren is the book imprint of
Poetry Wales Press Ltd
Nolton Street, Bridgend, Wales
www.seren-books.com

ISBN 1-85411-347-X

A CIP record for this title is available from
the British Library.

The publisher works with the financial assistance
of the Welsh Books Council.

Cover image: Lambert Photo, www.lambertphoto.com.

Printed in Plantin by Bell & Bain, Glasgow.

CONTENTS

INTRODUCTION
Sam Boardman-Jacobs

The contributors to this book vary in age and experience. Each of them has been influenced by differing periods of radio-drama listening. Each has gone on to make a major contribution to radio-drama writing. Between us all we encompass nearly fifty years of radio-drama history. This is not a book about a now-closed period of history. British radio-drama still thrives. According to BBC received wisdom, its audiences are getting older. Yet observation tells us that its writers are getting younger. One of the functions of this book is to tell would-be radio writers what the environment is like today; which 'slots' they can pitch their work at; and what the job feels like.

The golden days are gone when an aspiring radio-drama writer could be nurtured 'in-house' and encouraged until they finally came up with the goods. I was one of those privileged wannabees. Then, one was allowed failures on the path to success. I flowered, learnt my craft and made my name under that system. It is no more. Now, you have to get it right first time or there is no second time. Even so, as it did for me, radio-drama today can still provide a path which can lead through soaps and single plays to television and beyond. Joe Orton, Samuel Beckett, Tom Stoppard, Anthony Minghella, Louise Page, each has either started their drama career or made a major impact in the field of British radio-drama.

The contributors to this book are the living exponents of today's British radio-drama. It is noticeable how many of them have worked for, or have been influenced by Radio 4's *The Archers*. *The Archers* has been the training ground, or the mode of entry, for many a contemporary radio dramatist. Mick Martin, Louise Page, Christopher Hawes, Sue Teddern and I have all been *Archers* scriptwriters, and David Ian Neville has produced the programme. This is not indicative of nepotism on the editor's part; rather it is a tribute to the hunger of a soap, be it radio or television, for new writers, who, once trained tend to want to move on to less structured writing.

Mick Martin, as well as giving a useful day-to-day guide of what an *Archers* scriptwriter actually does, also shows the poignancy of being an ex-*Archers* writer. His piece is also a tribute to the team effort that makes a long running daily radio soap work:

> It's ever so slightly galling to discover that when you leave there is a sense in which nobody really notices. For individual writers may come and go, but the team goes on and on. The programme doesn't suddenly deteriorate, it doesn't grind to an ignominious halt, it doesn't lose thousands of listeners, and there are no letters to *Feedback* from listeners demanding to know where you've gone. All that happens is that when people trip over you skulking behind the aspidistra at parties, they slap you metaphorically on the back and say, 'Aren't you the bloke who used to write *The Archers?*'... before quickly passing on to find someone more interesting to talk to.

Penny Leicester, David Ian Neville and Tanya Nash all have useful tips for the aspiring radio writer from the producer's, director's and commissioning editor's point of view. Taken as a whole, their contributions add up to a three-dimensional picture of what a producer expects from today's radio writers.

Tanya Nash has good advice on how to relate to, and work with, your producer:

> A good producer will help you find the way to say what you want to write rather than impose their interpretation on your material. For this reason, I remind you to know what your play is about and its themes. At times your ideas will not be clear, but if you know what inspired them, then the producer can help you portray your vision.

Penny Leicester tells us that, far from being a deadening force, a producer's wisdom can open up the radio-drama horizons for a new writer. Penny believes, as do many of us, that radio-drama is still a powerful force in today's world of multiple communications:

> Nothing is impossible: a lump of rock can philosophise on the ages of man; a child can speak to its mother from the womb; the writer

can take the listener to the Battle of Waterloo or to the spaceship Mir without bankrupting the budgets. But, to me, radio's greatest strength is its ability to creep up on a listener and shake him or her to the core. In a time when we have become anaesthetised by television images of violence, war, deprivation, displacement and famine, in a time where celebrities front campaigns in order to shake us out of compassion fatigue, radio is, I believe, the most influential and powerful of all the media in that it speaks directly to the individual. It can break down barriers by raising awareness and promoting tolerance and understanding. (In the wrong hands, it can be used to devastating effect.)

Although this book contains much practical advice and information, it also attempts to give a holistic portrait of the way the history and development of radio has influenced the people who now write for it. Christopher Hawes remembers the Charles Parker Radio Ballads. These 'ballads' (dramatic narratives constructed from actuality recordings of working class life linked with folk music), and the political and social revolution of the late nineteen forties that influenced and created them, inspired Christopher's first major radio play. *The Snow Field* tells of a post-war working class poet and his discovery by a radically minded woman producer from the BBC in Manchester. The play contains some extremely interesting insights into that world of drama. It portrays the conflicts between the essentially middle class, radical producer and the self-educated, working class poet. It deals dramatically with the creation of both new writers and audiences for radio-drama.

Parker and (Euan) McColl created what amounted to a fresh radio art form. John Axon, a steam-train engine driver, had died in his cab because he stayed with his runaway train to try and warn the signal man of the train he was rushing towards. The Ballad is an elegy to his name, eliding taped voices of John Axon's work mates, friends and family in his hometown of Stockport into McColl and Seeger's eclectic score, mixing folk rhythms with jazz and calypso.

"You give her water, you give her coal
Hand on the regulator, watch her roll,
Mama, I swear, as long as I live
Gonna serve the steam locomotive.

Mama, listen to my narrative
Gonna serve the steam locomotive..."

Too often we take for granted what already is. Christopher Hawes shows us that radio-drama has always been and always will be in a state of flux and growth. Far too frequently, aspiring new writers submit rehashes of what already exists. Radio producers, like their counterparts in television, theatre and film, rarely know what they want next. It is the new dramatist who presents them with the future.

Louise Page is best known for her stage plays, now set texts in university drama department courses. Louise began her career in radio-drama, and it is interesting that, when her plays were criticised, the critics often accused her (quite wrongly I feel) of writing radio plays for the stage. What Louise has to say about the single play in radio-drama is also a good answer to all those people who waylay writers with their announcement that they have 'a great idea for a play':

> The most vital tool that any writer has is something to say. Writing
> is a superb form of arrogance. We expect other people to give up
> their money, and, more importantly in this day and age, their time,
> to listen to our ideas. For this reason, we owe them a structure.
> Writing a single play is not like telling your friends about a peculiar
> thing that happened to you in a restaurant: it's about creating a
> world for them and letting them feel part of it.

The contributors to this book, although they cannot 'teach' you structure, can point you in the right direction.

Nick McCarty is well known for his dramatisations of novels for radio-drama. He reveals to us that his task is not just a straightforward one of transposing novel dialogue to radio script dialogue:

> In *HMS Ulysses*, by Alistair MacLean, I was desperately casting
> around, trying to find a way to give the full power of the descriptions
> of what happened in that wonderful epic about a ship going on the
> deadly dangerous journey to Murmansk during the Second World
> War. MacLean had written this, his first book, out of deep knowledge
> and with a sort of passion that I had to try to translate to radio.
>   The solution was at once odd and at the same time very satisfying.
> The ship was given its own voice. Indeed, before the titles, Ulysses
> speaks some lines of a poem that is printed before the first chapter of
> the book. It is remarkable, but in this way Ulysses came alive for me
> and the terror of the storms and the encounters with the German Wolf
> Pack submarines was given a rich sense of place and event through
> the slightly epic voice of the ship on her last, desperate journey.

Ships that speak. Working-class history sung in ballad form. Radio-drama history proves it to be not just exercises in dramatic naturalism.

When I began writing for radio-drama, the prize, the aimed for and coveted 'slot', was the 90-minute Monday night play. This slot encouraged experiment and innovation. I was lucky – I wrote most of my early plays for Monday evening. But because the slot has now vanished, it does not follow that innovation and experiment in radio-drama have vanished also. The contemporary British radio play is usually 45 minutes in length. A few are 60 minutes. Most of the BBC radio-drama you will hear is naturalistic in form. It does not have to be so. The groundwork has already been done. I would urge new radio writers to attempt the impossible. A radio-drama producer can always 'tone down' your wild abstract concept. Producers find it harder to inject life into a timid and dull radio script.

As a teacher of scriptwriting, I constantly urge students to 'explore the view from your corner'. Working in a fish and chip shop may be dull if you have spent most of your life doing it. But the radio-drama audience does not know your 'normality'. They will be as fascinated by the back stage goings on in the 'chippie' as they would be by the worlds of high finance or high espionage. There is poetry and metaphor in the chip shop, as there is in the building society office. Most of us live in a multi-cultural, multi-ethnic world. There is no longer just history, there are histories. The world of drama is no longer monopolised by the doings of middle-aged white men. Radio-drama can be the truly democratic medium. Radio-drama, because of the size of its output, is ideally suited to showing ourselves to ourselves. Perhaps we are just nosy by nature. We love to look into other worlds, other lives.

Radio-drama, like the novel, exists in the mind of the listener. It is a truism to say that the pictures we can create in our heads are beyond bettering. Nevertheless it is a truth. We have to take care because of this. Several years ago, a radio thriller featured a scene of someone being tortured with an electric drill. On film, this would have been recreated with visual special effects. We are used to seeing horror simulated in the cinema. We are in a comforting group whose joint reactions we use to soften the impact. We are accustomed to visual horror. The very 'reality' of the scene adds a distance. In this particular radio play, all that was used was the sound effect of the drill and the recipient's scream, rapidly faded out. The BBC received a huge number of complaints about this scene. Each listener created their own mind picture of the event. Most of the audience found that image too terrifying to cope with. So, be cautious! Take the listener to the stars, but beware of taking them to their darkest nightmares.

So, how do radio writers work? A good but complex question, and one that this book attempts to answer. Radio writers come in all ages, shapes and sizes. In gathering together a representative selection, I have tried to cover all angles of the craft. However nothing is totally comprehensive. The most important element of this book is missing, it has to be. It does not yet exist. The most important element is you, the radio dramatist of the future. I hope that this book will enable you to draw on the lessons of the past and thus begin to create the radio dramas of the future. Several times in the book writers dwell on the many death notices that radio-drama has received. Like Mrs Blossom, a character who, in the less researched days of *The Archers*, was buried three times, radio-drama still springs back to life and relevancy. It is yours for the taking. Take it, and make it live for yet another generation!

THE WRITERS

THE SINGLE RADIO PLAY
Louise Page

Radio is not the place for plays that have failed to find homes in other mediums. Too often, frustrated writers have come to me, scripts in hand, saying, 'No one will accept this, so I thought I'd try it as a radio play,' without realising what an insult this is to one of the most difficult and creative dramatic forms. This is not to say that plays with a proven track record will not succeed on radio; but the medium is not a dumping ground for work that has been badly written and lacks ideas.

The single radio-play comes in many forms. It can follow the conventional three act structure, or it can jump backwards and forwards in time and space. The narrative can be carried by a single, internal voice, or divided between a group of characters and their interactions with one another. These sound like wonderful freedoms, but they are limited by the fact that radio is an entirely aural medium. The writer can provide no quick-fix visual interpretations of what is happening, for example the image of Hamlet behind the arras, the burning of Eilert Loevborg's manuscript by Hedda Gabler, Vladimir and Estragon waiting endlessly besides their tree. These visual situations provide potent metaphors in the theatre; they convey a situation before anyone has said anything. There is a scientific reason for this. Light moves faster than sound, so we see before we hear. Unless our sight is impaired, we learn very early on to interpret the world from its visual signals. It is now scientifically proven that in interpersonal relationships, a large percentage of information comes from body language, a smaller amount from tone of voice, and only a tiny percentage from the actual words used. Thus radio writing is a very imprecise form of communication. So, how does the writer of the single play use his or her dramatic capacity of thirty percent?

The most vital tool that any writer has is something to say. Writing is a superb form of arrogance. We expect other people to give up their money, and, more importantly in this day and age, their time, to listen to our ideas. For this reason, we owe them a structure. Writing a single play is not like telling your friends about a peculiar thing that happened to you in a restaurant: it's about creating a world for them and letting them feel part of it. Sound and subject matter go hand in hand.

To illustrate this in more detail, I plan to concentrate on two of my original radio plays, *The Prisoner Of Papa Stour* and *Working Out*. The genesis of the first was a holiday I spent in the Shetland Isles – windy, remote spots of land off the north coast of Scotland. I had been talking to the landlady of my bed-and-breakfast about the history of the islands, and one particularly wet and horrible day she brought me a box of old letters to read. These laid before me the story of Edwin Lindsay, who was known as 'The Prisoner of Papa Stour'. Lindsay was one of the sons of the Earl Balcarres and obviously suffered from some sort of mental illness, probably schizophrenia. To stop him being an embarrassment in society, he was sent to live on the tiny island of Papa Stour, where a travelling missionary, Maria Watson, was introduced to him. She managed to convince herself and others that Lindsay was being held captive against his will and determined to rescue him. After a couple of abortive attempts which were thwarted by Lindsay himself and his desire to return to Papa Stour, Maria and her captive arrived in London, where a court case was held regarding Lindsay's inheritance and his right not to be detained against his will. Though he lost the financial aspect of the case, Lindsay was not returned to Papa Stour but went to live with a doctor in Edinburgh, where he named landmarks around him after those he had known on the island.

These were the bare bones of the story which fascinated me. I asked myself time after time if Lindsay had wanted to be freed. Further research on the story revealed that during the 1820s and '30s, a time when the sea was the easiest form of transport, Papa Stour was far less isolated than we consider it to be now. There are accounts of Lindsay talking to visitors in French and playing the violin for dances. Not the caged figure that is at first conjured up by his story. The fact that he named places in Edinburgh after sites on the island made me think he could not have been too unhappy there. After all, early settlers in America and Australia named places to remind them of home and loved ones. The other aspect of the story that I wanted to unravel was that of Maria Watson. What made a straw-hat maker from Dunstable near Luton decide to become a missionary in the Shetland Isles? (I have to admit that I come from a family one branch of which was involved in the Luton straw trade. There is another play lurking in the Luton Records Office which I have yet to unearth.) Did Maria Watson make it her mission to rescue Lindsay because she thought he was a captive in a hostile environment or because she wanted to marry him and get her hands on his money?

These were all questions I asked myself as the play took shape in my mind. From the beginning, I knew that I wanted to use the material to make a radio play. The medium would allow me to conjure up the seas around Papa Stour, the fog that can sweep down at any moment, and Lindsay and Watson's journey south. Part of the latter would be set on an early steam train, not historically accurate but to give the image of the momentum of their journey as they headed towards the trial in London and the point of no return.

It took eight years from the conception of the play until I sat down to write it. This was partly due to the pressure of other work but mostly because the play had not ripened in my mind. I went on batting the ideas backwards and forwards, read the reports of the trial, and fantasised about going to Papa Stour to see where Lindsay had lived. But it is very easy as a writer to do too much research, then to justify that research by cramming every known fact into the play. So I decided to create the island in my imagination, basing it on other small islands. I wanted to write a play which was about motivation and sense of place, not an historical documentary.

It is difficult to tell now what was the nature of the real Edwin Lindsay's madness. Some of the historical evidence points to him not to having been mad at all but being banished by his father after refusing to fight a duel in India; but I felt that the evidence of him going to reside with a doctor after the trial indicated that there was more to the story than his family's fear of dishonour.

Once I had been commissioned by the BBC World Service to write the play, the first problem I had to solve was 'putting a clock' on it. This is the expression I use when writing for establishing the time scale of a play and letting the audience know where they are in that time scale. Edwin Lindsay spent years on Papa Stour and it was important to convey that sense of time without someone saying, 'You have now been here more than twenty years'. So, the play starts with Lindsay and the children of the house he is staying in trying to time a minute by letting sand run through their hands. It is only when they announce that minute is up that we discover that Lindsay's watch, which they are using to tell the time, is broken. Lindsay's answer to this is that it is better not to know the length of an hour. The listener immediately knows that he has been wherever he is for a long time. Then we get the credits which tell us that the play is called *The Prisoner Of Papa Stour.* The scene is set in the first minute of the play. The device of the children comes back several times to convey the passing of time.

At the end of the play, when they are grown up, Lindsay is still sending them toys as if they are still children, illustrating his lack of grasp on reality. The play begins and ends with a distorted perspective of time. What I see as Maria Watson's point of view is summed up in the first conversation she has with Edwin Lindsay. He tells her that he hates the idea of going to London because he only has one pair of shoe buckles and they might be stolen.

MARIA	Mr Lindsay, if you were in your rightful position in society you would have many pairs of shoes and more pairs of buckles.
LINDSAY	Once I had shoes that were only made for dancing.
MARIA	And you will so again.
LINDSAY	They were not so suitable for dancing as my naked feet.
MARIA	Mr Lindsay, have you forgotten? It is only savages that dance with bare feet! I have come to save you from such practices.
LINDSAY	I am no savage, Miss Watson.
MARIA	Sir, you must let me rescue you. It is my duty!

This brief snatch of dialogue from the play gives the listener many pieces of information. The shoe buckles set the play in the past. Lindsay was once rich and had certain shoes for special occasions. He is quite happy, in his present situation, to dance bare-footed. Maria Watson believes she belongs to a civilised society, as does Lindsay.

When he says he is no savage, it forms a bond between them. She is determined to rescue him, whether he wants it or not. It is a case of making every line count in conveying information to the listener and pushing forward the narrative of the play.

Lindsay's mental disorder is a combination of frenzy and lucidity. This is put into perspective by the obsessional natures of the two other main protagonists of the play, Maria Watson and the man she enlists to help her, George Pilkington. The strength of both of these characters is that the story could have been told from their angle, had it not been the nature of Lindsay's 'madness' or lack of it that fascinated me.

George Pilkington was an army officer who turned pacifist after being forced out of the army. The reason for this exclusion was that, whilst on a tour of duty in the West Indies, he had appointed a black soldier as an officer, an unprecedented move which brought him massive disapprobation. Having left the army, he supported himself and his family by giving pacifist lectures. He was also a vegetarian before the word had entered the language. In the play, the scene that convinces him that he should help Lindsay is one where they argue about pacifism. In it, Lindsay thinks that Pilkington is the one who is mad.

LINDSAY	You are a liar, Mr Pilkington!
PILKINGTON	Why is it a lie to say that defensive war is unlawful to a Christian?
LINDSAY	Because war is a Christian principle.
HENDERSON	Sir, I do believe Edwin is right.
PILKINGTON	On what do you base your principle, Mr Lindsay?
LINDSAY	Do you tell me you are a man who would defend neither his kingdom, nor his king?
PILKINGTON	I would defend them with words and counter arguments. As we argue now, Mr Lindsay.
LINDSAY	Then you would be as weak as a woman!
HENDERSON	I would fight for Papa and Shetland to the death.
PILKINGTON	Then, sir, I say, you are not a Christian.
LINDSAY	But Mr Pilkington, if a man took his sword to your sister or your mother –
PILKINGTON	I should apply the same principle.
LINDSAY	I dispute with you, sir. You have seen Kirsty Henderson?

PILKINGTON	A very pretty child.
LINDSAY	Suppose I took my sword to her in the middle of dinner? What then?
PILKINGTON	I would wait for your conscience to stop you.
LINDSAY	What if my conscience did not stop me? If I was mad with drink or worse?
PILKINGTON	I would say if you had not touched drink or become intoxicated by the privileges of wearing a red coat, the circumstance would not have arisen.
HENDERSON	Edwin does not touch drink.
PILKINGTON	I am glad to hear it, Mr Henderson.
LINDSAY	Sir, you say all violence is un-Christian.
PILKINGTON	All violence. Even the defence of self.
LINDSAY	Then I accuse you of not valuing your life! You would be a man as guilty of self-destruction as any suicide! You would deserve to be buried at the most remote cross roads in the country.
PILKINGTON	Well said Mr Lindsay!

I wanted to use the scene to show that we can all be 'mad' on some occasions. Convinced by this conversation that Lindsay is rational, even though he has a totally different viewpoint, Pilkington determines that he will rescue Lindsay. As Pilkington sees it, Lindsay is a slave as much as other slaves that he battled to liberate in the past. He persuades him to leave the island and go to Lerwick, from where they can continue south. Unfortunately, while Pilkington is being ridiculed for giving a pacifist lecture to raise money for the journey to London, Lindsay is plied with drink and decides to return to Papa Stour. They return by open boat in the fog, having to smell their way back – a scene that would have been impossible in the theatre without swirling dry ice. In the radio play, the isolation of the sea is indicated by the fact that Henderson has to smell his way back to the island by the scent of the vegetation. In a page of scene, it was possible to convey the lonely vastness of the North Atlantic. Pilkington's lack of success in rescuing the prisoner leads to an estrangement between him and Maria Watson. She gets Lindsay off the island by constantly flattering him about his noble birth; and when she writes to him she very consciously signs her letters, 'Maria Watson, Miss.' Those four letters should convey to the audience the idea that she has a romantic reason for rescuing Lindsay.

Once Lindsay has been finally rescued and taken to London, the

argument between Pilkington and Watson continues. She is all for a
court case, he for turning the other cheek and forgiving his brother for
keeping him imprisoned. The obsession of these two protagonists is
shown by the way in which they bully Lindsay. Maria Watson
convinces him that a trial suing for his inheritance is the best way
forward, and though he wins the money, it is decided that he should
stay under medical care in Edinburgh.

Lindsay's voice is deliberately not heard at the end of the play. The
silence of the central character in the last three scenes of the play is used
to symbolise the fact that his so called 'rescuers' have cut him off from
all he knew and believed in. They are the ones who have imprisoned him.

Working Out is a very different type of play. It came from one
simple idea: the way in which outworkers were paid in the knitting
industry. I knew someone who knitted to sell to the garment industry
and was horrified to discover how little she got paid compared with the
shop mark up. The bubble burst when, in a scene echoed in the play,
she saw one of the jumpers she had knitted as part of a fashion article.
The markup was five times what she had been paid and her sense of
anger and pain was palpable.

I was also interested in how one could convey a visual act like
knitting on radio. Good knitting is a very rhythmic activity and a
decent knitter hardly has to look at what they are doing. It seemed that
the obvious way to convey this was in verse. Because I was using an
aural image to illustrate a visual skill, it was essential as a writer that I
set up the convention as soon as possible so that the listeners knew the
world I was asking them to inhabit. So, the play starts with Alison
knitting and imagining her daughter, Nettie's, reaction when she gives
her the special jumper she has knitted. This allowed me to set up the
craft of knitting and the fact that the play would use interior
monologue as a commentary on the action.

SFX OF KNITTING.

NETTIE   It's lovely, Mum, lovely. Brilliant. Smashing.
         I'll look like a peacock. Radiant. Dashing.
ALISON   Nettie, no one else will have a cardi like it.
NETTIE   Mum, I can't tell you, I'm delighted.
ALISON   A special present for a special girl.
NETTIE   Shall I put it on and do a twirl?
PAT   (*APP*) Alison, I don't know how you

know where you are with that knitting.
ALISON   You get into a rhythm, two pink, three green.
And the pattern continues while you dream.

In nine lines, underlaid with the sound effect of knitting, the audience is given the information that when a character in the play is knitting she speaks in verse, be it in her front room or on the bus. The other theme of the play that's set up in the first scene is the exploitation of workers that goes on in the garment trade. The reason Pat has come to see Alison is to show off a cheap outfit she has bought for a dinner dance. This theme is carried on through the play and, in the final scene between Nettie and Alison, Alison refuses to go to Turkey to exploit knitters there when they prove to be cheaper than English workers.

Nettie comes home and receives her jumper. Then, when she is shopping in Covent Garden, she is offered fifty pounds for it. She is tempted and, *Working Out* being a radio play, I could write in the devil coming and sitting on her shoulder.

SFX OF COFFEE SHOP IN COVENT GARDEN.

BABS   Annette, I'm offering you fifty pounds for a cardigan
         you've already worn.
NETTIE   Hardly worn.

THE DEVIL COMES AND SITS ON NETTIE'S SHOULDER.

DEVIL   Good.
NETTIE   Who are you?
DEVIL   You don't recognise me?
NETTIE   Sort of.
DEVIL   (RUSTLING BANK NOTES) I am the devil who sits
         on your shoulder and rubs the sound of money in your
         ears. That's the sound of money, not an overdraft.
BABS   Would you like another coffee while you think about it?
DEVIL   She knows what she wants, Nettie. What do you?
NETTIE   Yes, I'd love another one.
BABS   Waiter!
DEVIL   This is how it sounds in coins.

THE DEVIL PLAYS COINS THROUGH HIS HANDS.

NETTIE   Louder!

THE COINS BECOME LOUDER.

We know that Nettie has made her decision. She quickly goes into business, first with Babs and then on her own account, selling jumpers knitted by her mother and her mother's friends. In her desire to make more money, Nettie quickly gets into exploitation, until she can't hear the devil any longer but acts off her own bat. This quickly leads to her severing her relationships with all those around her and the play culminates in a scene with her mother, when the rift between them becomes irreconcilable.

Though *Working Out* and *The Prisoner Of Papa Stour* deal with much the same subject matter, that of people thinking they are doing good when they are actually doing harm, they are both written using very different techniques but exploiting the medium of radio. In *Papa Stour*, I had to create an historic world of coaches and boats and did this through a formality of speech. When I write plays set in the past, I try not to recreate dialogue but to give a flavour of something distanced from the way in which we talk now. My aim, as with the knitting in *Working Out*, is to create an atmosphere for the listener, so that they have a spatial feeling for the piece. Sometimes it can be hard to think of the right setting for a scene, and it wasn't until the second or third draft of *Working Out* I created the devil because I felt that the scene in which Nettie decides to sell her jumper needed more meat in it.

When both plays were finished and in studio, it became clear that, despite my best efforts to time them, they were too long. Fortunately, on both occasions I was at the recording and could frantically make cuts. Inevitably these were some of my favourite scenes; but when faced with a tight time slot, you cut as much as you can while still preserving the integrity of the work. I still miss some of the scenes from *The Prisoner of Papa Stour*, but, had I not cut them, things like the journey to London in the early train would have had to have been cut.

The thing that I find most frustrating about working in radio-drama is its ephemeral quality. Despite the medium's massive drama output, very little is ever reviewed, compared with the massive coverage given to television and theatre. It can feel that you are putting hours and hours of work into a play which hardly anyone is going to hear. The important thing is to keep faith with the listeners; to write with as much attention to detail and structure as one would when writing anything else; to keep the voice going by speaking out.

THE BLOKE WHO WROTE *THE ARCHERS*
Mick Martin

It always happens. You're at a party, and you find yourself in the corner of the room, just by the aspidistra that the hostess forgot to dust, deep in conversation with a stranger. It's only a matter of time before you have to face up to the inevitable question... 'And what do you do?' How can you put it? 'I'm a writer.' No – far too pompous. 'I work for the BBC'? No – ditto, and not strictly accurate. 'I'm a scriptwriter'? Makes it sound as if I've just flown in from Hollywood. 'I work at home'? Far too vague. 'I write soap'? Incomprehensible. Ultimately, there's nothing for it – take a deep breath and tell the truth. 'I'm a writer for *The Archers* on Radio 4.' Silence.

In the six years that I wrote for *The Archers*, it became apparent that the reaction that followed the silence almost inevitably fell into one of two broad categories. Number one was something loosely related to, but not quite equivalent to admiration. 'How wonderful!' my interlocutor would beam, before proceeding to broadcast (I use the term loosely) his or her discovery of just what he or she had come across beside the dusty aspidistra to as many of those present as possible. Ere long most people in the room would be aware that somewhere lurking in a corner was an *Archers* writer. Even those who had little or no idea what *The Archers* was would be pretty chuffed that they'd 'met' one of its creators. And it would be a safe bet that the next time I ventured out into a social context, there'd be someone there whose greeting would be to slap me metaphorically on the back and say 'Aren't you the bloke that writes *The Archers?*'

Category number two was quite different. No 'how wonderful' here, but the silence would be followed by a kind of grimace, as the face of the questioner settled into an attitude of embarrassed compassion, as if I had just revealed some awful personal tragedy. Nobody ever actually said, 'Oh, I am sorry.' But that's what they meant – you could see it. Their reasoning, presumably, was that writing is a noble art, that what every writer sets out to do is to create the great novel, play or poem. But here was this poor wretch, whose once lofty aspirations had come to nought and who now spent his days trying to grub a living in the literary gutters of a radio soap-opera... who in short was to be pitied.

Now I have no objection to admiration, and I can even put up with pity, in small quantities. But the fact is that during the conversations that would inevitably follow the initial expression of one or the other, it became clear that each was the product of fundamental misconceptions about how a soap writer works. Many, varied and bizarre, indeed, are the ideas that people have on the subject. In my time I met people who assumed I wrote the programme on my own, people who thought I wrote for just one character while other writers wrote for the rest, people who imagined that I wrote one of the scenes in each episode... and so on. None of these assumptions is true. So what does a soap writer actually do?

It was in November 1992 that I was finally invited to join *The Archers*. I say finally, because this was some eighteen months after I had originally applied. In response to that application, I had received a request to write a trial episode. And this had evidently been deemed good enough to secure me a meeting at Pebble Mill with the programme's editor, Vanessa Whitburn. I remember little about this meeting, except that it lasted a very long time, and that at one point Vanessa put a sheet of paper over the left hand side of my script, and said she liked the way that she could tell from the dialogue who was talking even without seeing the names. I obviously knew the programme and the characters. So I did! *The Archers* was first broadcast just a few days before I was born. And I had listened to it on and off ever since.

At the end of the interview, Vanessa said she'd put my name at the top of her list of reserve writers, and would contact me further within twelve months. My experience of the relationship between writers and theatre directors is such that I confidently expected this was the last I would ever hear. I was to learn, however, that in many ways writers are rather more valued on *The Archers* than they generally are in the theatre, and true to her word, almost twelve months to the day later, the call came. Would I like to join the programme?

My first duty thereafter was to attend a 'long-term storyline conference' – which was very appropriate, since these meetings, held twice a year, can be seen as the first step in the complicated process of putting the programme together. Some time before the meeting, each of the writers on the programme is 'invited' to submit two or three long-term story ideas, i.e. the bare bones of major long-running stories affecting the main characters and the future development of the programme. From the two-dozen or more submissions, the editor, in consultation with her producers, usually selects about half for discussion at the long-term storyline conference, which is attended by all the writers, the production team, the agricultural editor, and often one or more of the special advisers attached to the programme. As a result of what is often quite heated debate, inevitably a number of the ideas are thrown out. Very occasionally ideas are accepted largely as they stand – as the writer has conceived them. Far more often the effect of the discussion is to refine, develop and, not least importantly, to combine the ideas on the table, so that at the end of the day there are up to half a dozen storylines worked out in broad outline, that will feed into the programme over the coming period – a period that can range from six months up to as much as three or more years.

I learned a lot from this first long-term meeting – and I don't just mean that I found out what was going to happen in the programme over the next couple of years. Much more importantly, I learned that when working on a soap you are above all a member of a team. And this has a mass of implications. It means, for instance, that you need to leave your ego at home. After working for however long on your pet idea, you have to be able to cope with the fact that it may not even get to the table... or, far more distressingly, it may reach the table, only to be slagged off left right and centre in discussion, before being unceremoniously consigned to the waste-bin of great ideas that nobody else thought were great ideas. Even if your idea (usually in modified form) is accepted, it then passes into common ownership in a way that obviously doesn't happen when you're writing your own single play or series. You have to be prepared for others to work on the idea, and for it to be adapted/modified/developed in ways that you may not have intended and possibly don't agree with. And you have to reconcile yourself to the fact that with ten writers on the team, on average ninety percent of the drama that deals with what was once 'your' idea is going to be written by other people. The corollary of that, of course, is that part of what you have to write and make to 'work' may be the product of other people's ideas that you never thought would work in the first place.

All this leads to moments of frustration. But being a member of a team is not all bad news. In this case, what I was joining was a group of people who *had* learned how to leave their egos at home. Certainly they might slag off each other's *ideas*; but they didn't slag each *other* off. Certainly they argued their corner vigorously; but they were also prepared to listen to the arguments of others. The point was, of course, that we were all in the same boat. We were all prone to the same frustrations. We all felt similarly vulnerable. And we were all equally aware that the only way to get the job done was to deal with the frustration and vulnerability and to work by co-operation rather than confrontation. The ability to write was of course an important qualification for being on the team. But the ability to get on with other members of the team was ultimately an even more important one. It would be disingenuous to suggest that everything was sweetness and light all the time. But in general what had emerged was an uncommonly loyal and supportive working environment.

After the long-term storyline conference, the next stop was that month's (unimaginatively named) short-term storyline conference. These are held every four weeks, and again present are the editor, producers and all the writers, four of whom will be paying particular attention since it will be their task to write the scripts for the four weeks under discussion. Prior to the meeting, each of the writers receives a writers' pack which includes a reminder of where each of the storylines currently running has got to, and suggestions, worked out by the production staff, as to how they might develop further, which act as a spur to discussion. Normally there will be a dozen or more storylines running at a given time. These include the major stories fed into the programme as a result of long-term storyline conference discussion in the past. There are also a number of middle-term stories, often taking elements from long-term suggestions made in the past. And there are short-term stories, which arrive in a manner that I never wholly understood, but which seems to work well enough. The atmosphere of this meeting is a good deal more concentrated and structured. The different storylines are discussed individually, the objective being to come away after eight hours with a detailed plan of exactly how each is going to be developed week by week.

To this end, the discussion has to strike an extraordinary balance between allowing the freedom for creativity and achieving the focus necessary to avoid waffle and get through the agenda. The result is a rather curious hybrid – a kind of rampant democracy, in which all present contribute to the discussion and effectively determine its outcome by consensus, is carefully contained within a kind of benevolent autocracy imposed by the chairperson (usually the editor), to stop the discussion of particular topics veering off up blind alleys or dragging on long after it has ceased to be useful. And there is a sense in which this tension between creativity and restriction is the key to the existence of the soap writer. Certainly he or she is encouraged to be creative, as much and sometimes more than the writer of individual plays. But there are limits to that creativity – and those limits are defined once again by the needs of the team as a whole.

If that sounds like bad news, the good news is that the short-term storyline conference reveals the team to be much larger than you first thought. And any inclination that a writer may have to feel slightly disgruntled at the restrictions imposed by being a member of a team is very quickly overcome by the realisation that, by and large, other members of the team will be doing the bulk of your research for you. The efforts of the production staff and programme advisers are nowhere more apparent than in the research notes that accompany the storylines in each month's writers' pack. Detailed notes from the Agricultural Editor outline exactly what is happening on farms and in the world of agriculture during the period in question. And these are supplemented by equally detailed notes relating to individual storylines. Thus, if there's a legal story running, there is a complete account of the legal processes involved. When one of the characters underwent IVF treatment, there was a mass of material on the medical, emotional and legal aspects of that. When one of the characters did a line-dancing class, there was a sheaf of papers about line-dancing. One of the lesser known advantages of being a soap writer indeed is that you come away with a vast, if eclectic, body of knowledge about a huge variety of subjects ranging from the very serious to the very silly – which would be very useful at parties, incidentally, if only people didn't keep wanting you to talk about your job.

After about six months apprenticeship attending the monthly

short-term meetings, the day came when I was one of the four writers commissioned to write for that month. Nothing like the prospect of making your debut to concentrate the mind. Many and detailed were the notes I took on the discussions that took place that day. But I wasn't the only one. Script meetings always take place on a Monday, and on the Thursday I received from the office a copy of that month's detailed, week-by-week storyline outline – the product of the discussions that had taken place three days earlier. In the section that related to the week I was writing was an exact account of precisely what should happen in my week in each of the storylines running. In the case of the major stories, these were relatively complicated. In the case of minor stories the description might only run to a couple of lines indicating how the story should be progressed and 'kept alive'.

What followed were the four worst days of my professional life. Receiving the storylines on a Thursday I had until the following Tuesday morning to come up with a detailed scene-by-scene synopsis of the (in those days) five episodes I would eventually write. Sounds easy? Well, it isn't. Here one is furthest away from the life of a 'normal' writer. Any creativity involved is that of a crossword-puzzle solver rather than a writer, as you look for ways in which the different stories will fit together and overlap, so that you can cram this mass of material into the 75 available minutes of radio-drama. And nowhere are the restrictions more apparent. The most obvious have to do with the notion of structure. You have to plan the week so that the major stories are progressed in clear stages and at an even pace throughout the five days. Along the way, you have to remember that each individual episode needs to end on some kind of 'hook' that will make the listener want to tune-in the next day. And once you have established a structure for the major stories, you have to fit the minor ones, which almost inevitably involve different characters, around it.

The less obvious restrictions have to do with the fact of working for radio. Number one is that any programme has to operate within a budget, which means that there is a curb on the number of characters you can use. The budget restricts casting to an average of seven characters per episode. If you use more than seven in any given episode, you have to 'save' one from one of the other episodes that week. That's not all. Restriction number two comes from the fact that the drama needs to make clear sense on the radio... which it won't if, for instance, a given character is heard at the end of one scene in a given location, and then also used in a different location and at a different time at the opening of the next scene. 'Jump cuts' need to avoided and, in the case of *The Archers* in particular, since the programme has an omnibus edition on a Sunday morning as well as the daily episodes, you even have to remember (restriction number three) to expunge any possible jump cuts between the final scene of one episode and the first scene of the next. When planning your synopsis, you also have to remember the need for variety – of location (three consecutive scenes in different characters' kitchens quickly becomes tedious), of tone (if you're pursuing a 'heavy' or tragic storyline, you'll need something lighter within that episode to create balance), even of length of scene (too many consecutive short scenes can be bitty, consecutive long scenes can be boring). And not least of your considerations is the need to bring the characters and the drama to life on the radio. Except in particular circumstances and for specific reasons, scenes in which people 'just talk' tend to make for extremely bland listening and don't work. What exactly is going on in this scene, you have to keep asking yourself – and how can it (ideally) contribute to, or *(faute de mieux)* complement, what I am trying to make the scene do?

And then of course there's that other category of restrictions – those that come from being part of a team. You have to liaise very closely with the writers who are writing the other weeks in that month. It is vital that, as the four writers simultaneously plan their weeks, they each remain aware of what the others are doing. If you're writing the third week, you cannot finalise the way you are going to treat a major story until you have some idea of how it will have been treated by whoever is writing the second week. So, there are constant phone calls to your colleagues to ensure continuity, and once again there's no place in these conversations for ego or preciousness.

Four days, numerous screwed-up pieces of paper, umpteen cups of coffee and doses of paracetamol later, you breathe a sigh of relief, e-mail your synopsis to the office, and retire exhausted to the pub/bed or wherever. At that point, you'd be glad never to hear of *The Archers* or of your synopsis again. Trouble is, you do. Three days later comes a phone call from the editor (or whoever is co-ordinating the script editing process that month) to discuss and refine your synopsis, requesting changes where necessary. Unless you have made some kind of cock-up (which can happen if you're working quickly) there shouldn't be major structural changes requested. But often minor changes are necessary to ensure that the continuity of the programme is maintained, not only (most obviously) in terms of narrative logic, but also in terms of emotional development and the way in which given stories are treated.

Following this round of phone calls, each writer is sent a copy of the synopsis of the other three, along with details of the changes that have been requested. And at this point the structure and content of the month's episodes are effectively set in stone. Any creativity now is restricted to the writing of the dialogue. If you suddenly start being 'creative' in other areas at this point, the whole scheme of things is likely to collapse. You have about ten days to write the episodes for your week. In one sense this is not all that onerous: you've done the hard work, and what is left is simply to supply the dialogue for the structure that you have already established in detail. On the other hand, 75 minutes' worth of dialogue in ten days is a lot. And the pressure this exerts undoubtedly is a burden. You can't wake up one morning and decide you don't feel like it. You can't 'do it tomorrow'. You can't wait for inspiration. You can't take the weekend off because the sun is shining and you want to sit on the beach. As the partners of regular soap writers are apt to confirm, often with some feeling, during this ten day period you can't do anything much – except write.

Eleven days later, the finished scripts are dispatched to arrive on a Tuesday, exactly two weeks after the submission of the synopsis, and three weeks and one day after the script meeting that set this whole process in motion. For three days there is silence, as the scripts are read. Then on the Friday, a further phone call from the editor reveals which scenes, if any, need to be re-written. Because the system that has evolved over the years is as detailed as it is, and because everyone involved tends to do his or her job properly, the number of 're-writes' requested is generally remarkably small. Where they are requested, it is often merely minor points of structure or tone that need attention. In the rare cases where more significant problems do occur, it is often because the writer has found him or herself having to deal with a story that he or she didn't particularly like in the first place. I experienced this in the case of one incident that landed up in a week I had to write.

I had argued unsuccessfully against its inclusion and I had never thought it was a good idea. After having several goes at it during the normal writing period, I had to re-write the relevant scene... not once, as it turned out, but twice. Even after that, when it was broadcast, it sounded like a scene written by someone who still wasn't entirely convinced it could be made to work. You have the weekend to do the re-writes. And that, finally, is the end of the writing process... At least it would be, except that by the time you've done them, of course, it's Monday... and not just any old Monday, but the day of the next short-term script conference. Twenty-eight days have elapsed since the process began, and it's about to begin all over again. And because you remain part of the ongoing process, once you have done your re-writes, your involvement with the scripts you have just written effectively comes to an end. These will be recorded in studio during the next month (while you may be busy writing your next batch of scripts.) And while writers are encouraged to attend recordings, the tightness of the scheduling means that there is little opportunity at this stage for much active input. Certainly there is no time for the sort of detailed discussions of interpretation that one would normally have with the director and actors in the case of a single play. The fact is that you have passed 'your' scripts on to other members of the team... and it will be another month before you discover, when the episodes are broadcast, the extent to which your enforced trust in them has been justified.

So... the short answer to the question, 'What does a soap writer actually do?' is that (s)he contributes in a number of clearly defined ways to a collaborative process that gets the programme made. As such, the individual soap writer, should you happen to meet one, is probably neither to be admired nor to be pitied. Yes, there are some 'wonderful' aspects to the job. *The Archers* enjoys a very high profile, and what you write is listened to and discussed by millions of people. If you're lucky, you might write something that influences, moves, amuses and entertains millions of people, which won't be the case for the writer of a single play. And yes, there are some counts on which you deserve sympathy. What you write is severely restricted by your membership of a team, and by a number of outside constraints, and even when it works it isn't really wholly yours... which also isn't the case for the writer of a single play. But ultimately the point is that the individual is emphatically not the point... it is the team that is important. You're reminded of this at every stage of the work that you do while you're with the programme. And it's forcibly brought home to you again when you decide to leave, as I did at the end of 1998. It's ever so slightly galling to discover that when you leave there is a sense in which nobody really notices. For individual writers may come and go, but the team goes on and on. The programme doesn't suddenly deteriorate, it doesn't grind to an ignominious halt, it doesn't lose thousands of listeners, and there are no letters to *Feedback* from listeners demanding to know where you've gone. All that happens is that when people trip over you skulking behind the aspidistra at parties, they slap you metaphorically on the back and say, 'Aren't you the bloke who used to write *The Archers?*'... before quickly passing on to find someone more interesting to talk to.

HEADS AND TAILS
Nick McCarty

'Begin at the beginning, go to the end, and then stop.'

I began dramatising novels for radio with a seven-hour version of *A Tale Of Two Cities*. I suppose it would be fair to say I jumped in at the deep end: a well known book; films, theatre and television versions by the score; and an ending so well known and so maudlin that it makes the modern reader wince. 'It is a far, far better thing... etc., etc.' Impossible to do without reducing the audience to guffaws of laughter.

It was whilst I was writing the script for this serial that I came to certain conclusions about the way to approach the task of translating another author's work into a totally different medium. Radio and the novel do however have one thing in common – by and large they address an audience of one, and that is important.

I should stress that this is not a primer, nor is it a collection of short-cuts to adapting classic books for radio. It is a pull-together of some aspects of the work that are important to me.

Dickens one might expect to be easier to adapt than most because he wrote in episodes for the magazine market. I assumed that I'd find the 'joins', and so the problem of episode breaks would be made easier to solve. But I found it impossible, on reading the novel, to discover the 'natural breaks'. His skill of course.

So, how do I begin? First I make a chapter by chapter précis of the book. I try to make these breakdowns as full as possible. This does two things: it gives me a very clear understanding of the structure of the work; and it also gives me a sense of the balance of characters and the balance of the dramatic action.

At this point I should say that I do not believe in rewriting the original work. If it's worth adapting, it will usually have stood the test of time or quality, and people will be listening in order to hear the voice of Dickens, or Hardy or D.H. Lawrence, or Kazantzakis, or whoever.

It is certainly not the adapter's voice they want to hear. There is a school of thought that feels it's fine to add chunks of new material, to make characters do things they do not do in the original. Most of the reasons for this have to do with making the material sexier, more easily digestible. If adapters choose to go that route, then that's up to them; but it's a route I'd rather not go down.

So, you have the scene-by-scene, chapter-by-chapter breakdown, and you have been given enough space in terms of episodes to do the work without skimping. You can't do *A Tale Of Two Cities* in four hours and call it *A Tale Of Two Cities*. It would inevitably be a pastiche. It would mean, for example, cutting minor characters to the bone. And that would make my method almost impossible, because I need those minor characters.

The translation to radio from the page means an inevitable loss of texture. Descriptions of place, mood or people may be lost; relationships glossed over; thoughts ignored; unless you can find a way to incorporate them into the grammar of the script and your way of telling the story. The minor characters can often solve that problem. They may be hovering on the edges of scenes, not given a voice by the novelist, but they are there, seeing events and action as they happen, and it may be quite easy to give them a voice. When it is possible to go into the mind of the major character, however – to discover their thoughts, attitudes and mood – that needs to be set up very early in the adaptation.

Through such devices we 'see' the main protagonists. Through them we become intimate with the places in which the action takes place. Thus, in a short adaptation of *Love Among The Haystacks*, which was written as part of a group of three plays from D.H. Lawrence short stories, a decision was made to use the same 'voice' to carry the descriptive narrative line. In that case, who better than Lawrence, whose lyric descriptions did not sit happily in the mouths of his farm labouring characters?

Using Lawrence's voice to open the scene tells us not only where the characters are and what they are doing; it also quickly sets up the edge between the two brothers. This speed is essential in a piece that only has forty-five minutes to run. There is no time for the more relaxed style of *The Water Gypsies* for example:

DHL:	*The two fields lay on a hillside facing south. Being newly cleared of hay, they were golden green. The stack was being built, massive but so silvery and delicately bright that it seemed to have no weight. The two brothers were waiting for another load on the wagon. They stood wiping their brows from the heat. They moved, from time to time, packing the hay down and riding higher over the hedge tops on the stack.*
MAURICE:	By it's hot enough.
DHL:	*Maurice was the younger brother. Handsome, careless. A man who often seemed as if aroused... passionate even.*
GEOFFREY:	Did tha see her again. Maurice?
MAURICE:	Who?
GEOFFREY:	Who? Tha knows damn well who. Her over the elderflower. I' the vicar's garden. The white haired un. Her.
DHL:	*Geoffrey was a hulking man of twenty two. He was sensitive; inexperienced... jealous as he watched his brother standing leaning his chin on the smooth pommel of his fork, looking away across the faint haze to the blue heap of Nottingham. Across the land smoke from the colliery wove a path. There was a silence by the old church and the trees.*

In *HMS Ulysses*, by Alistair MacLean, I was desperately casting around, trying to find a way to give the full power of the descriptions of what happened in that wonderful epic about a ship going on the deadly dangerous journey to Murmansk during the Second World War. MacLean had written this, his first book, out of deep knowledge and with a sort of passion that I had to try to translate to radio.

The solution was at once odd and at the same time very satisfying. The ship was given its own voice. Indeed, before the titles, Ulysses speaks some lines of a poem that is printed before the first chapter of the book. It is remarkable, but in this way Ulysses came alive for me and the terror of the storms and the encounters with the German Wolf Pack submarines were given a rich sense of place and event through the slightly epic voice of the ship on her last, desperate journey.

1. Hear the whining keening howling wind off the Arctic wastes. Far distant at first and then coming closer and building with the sea

> as we hear ULYSSES (the voice of the ship) giving us part of the
> Tennyson poem. It stops dead...
> 2. STOKER RILEY refuses a direct order. He has had enough and
>   so have the rest of them... Other sailors refuse orders.
> 3. And the clatter of many men on metal steps and the shouting of
>   orders and a PROVOST SGT shouting at a closed door if they
>   don't come out hands up and no trouble he is sending the
>   Marines to sort them out...

In *A Tale of Two Cities*, one of the minor characters sits outside a
solicitor's office in the City of London. His job is to run errands and
take messages for the clerks and principals in the office. Thus he sees
everything and everybody, and is trusted by the people who use him.
He is a richly comic invention with a wife who is 'forever a floppin' and
a prayin' and I won't have it...' And he needs his wife's prayers, for he
is a resurrection man: he takes bodies from graves so that surgeons
may teach their trade. It is through this comic and terrifying character
that we get eyewitness descriptions of the men and women whom
Dickens draws so richly.

I have called this essay 'Heads and Tails' for a simple reason. If you
can get them right, you have gone a long way to solving the problems
of the dramatisation. Heads, or the openings, of any adaptation need to
perform a number of services. They show us where, they tell us when,
and they inform us about the nature of the story we are telling over the
next 45 minutes or the next five hours. There is a common need, I
believe, for both the adapter and the listener to feel that he or she
knows the grammar of this kind of storytelling.

Take the opening of *The Strange Case Of Doctor Jekyll And Mr Hyde*.
The opening directions set a number of things before a word is spoken:
the song should tell us something of the period; the noise of the pub
tells us that it's a free and easy sort of a place; and then the action kicks
in as the chair crashes to the floor and glasses shatter and voices are
raised in anger. We hear through the raised voices a voice we will come
to know. Hyde roars in anger at a girl and is grossly offensive. Then we
hear that he has a bottle of acid and is about to blind the girl or maim
her... which he duly does. The scene ends on a terrible racking scream
from the girl, and we mix from that shocking vileness...

This is an opening full of menace and terror which provides us with
a knowledge about Hyde (played wonderfully by Michael Maloney)

that the other characters do not have until the very end of the piece. It was not an easy show to get right and David Hitchinson directed it with great elegance.

A MAN:	(ANGRY) That's my girl you're talking to. You mind your manners.
GIRL:	(CRYING) He said... he said awful things to me Charlie.
MAN:	Is that right? I'll kick your head in you... you...
HYDE:	(AMUSED) You... you and your slut. I only asked her price you pimp.
MAN:	(FURIOUS) I'll swing for you.
ANOTHER MAN:	Watch him Charlie... His pocket...
HYDE:	See if she likes this... eh...
WOMAN:	(TERRIFIED) The stink of it. It's acid girl... watch your eyes!
GIRL:	(ACROSS HER) No!
HYDE:	Spoil your pretty face for you... melt it for you... Here... try it.

THERE IS A TERRIBLE RACKING SCREAM AND CHAOS.

THE MOURNFUL HOOTING OF A RIVER BOAT IN A FOG. THE DISTANT SOUND OF A HORSE-DRAWN CARRIAGE. A DOOR OPENS AS SOMEONE ENTERS A HOUSE OF THE STREET.

LANDLADY:	(EMERGING FROM HER ROOM) Is that you Mr Hyde?
HYDE:	(HISSING WITH EFFORT) Yes. Any callers?
LANDLADY:	None. Here... you're cut Mr Hyde, about the face and...
HYDE:	Nothing. (ON STAIRS) Goodnight.
LANDLADY:	Did you hear about the girl in the Turks Head? Terrible.
HYDE:	Really?
LANDLADY:	A man threw acid over her... A small man... they said.. Bearded man they said... they said...

The Water Gypsies by A.P. Herbert, on the other hand, is quiet, gentle and charming. Jane is on intimate terms with us from the moment she opens her mouth. We know she's full of romance and fun, and that her sister Lily is perhaps a little more racy. By the end of that first page we know a great deal about the background of the main character and about how she lives, about her dreams and her hopes, and about her down-to-earth sense of reality. Played in the right way, this gives the perfect sense of what is to come; and Amanda Root got it just right.

> HEAR JANE VERY CLOSE TO US. SHE WILL USE THIS DEVICE OF TALKING TO US DIRECTLY FROM TIME TO TIME.

JANE:	Oh, I loved the pictures. Roman Novarro, the desert Sheik, Valentino. My sister, Lily, liked him best of all. All romance and hot kisses and sin.
LILLY:	Look at him... Look at him Jane. Look at his eyes. Lovely eyes.
LILLY:	Can you see dad... is he in the pit?
JANE:	He was practising last night. The cello part. Here it comes.

> AND IT DOES. MUSIC SWELLS A TOUCH AND

ANNOUNCER:	*The Water Gypsies* by A.P. Herbert. Adapted for radio in six parts by Nick McCarty. Part one: Destined for better things.
JANE:	Better than the flicks I like the river. The old Thames by Hammersmith Bridge swirling by all brown and yellow after a flood. Like silk. Lovely. And sailing... I love to sail our old dinghy. Not that I get much time. Now with seeing after Lilly and dad and the old barge we live on. Not since I came to work... live-in maid of all work... Jane Bell. Me.

We also know, of course, that the character we will be following is a young and delightful girl living in rather a bohemian way. With luck the audience is intrigued enough to want to keep with the story.

This challenge of hooking the audience is important, and there seem to be as many theories and didactic statements about it as about anything else. Some dramatists look to provide rapid, noisy action: the car crash, the row, the emotional crescendo – often ideas torn from TV or the opening title sequences of movies. My route is usually quieter, more character-and location-led than action-led. Horses, no doubt, for courses; but this is my preference, whatever the material.

HMS Ulysses opens quietly enough at an Admiralty board of enquiry. But it seemed to me and to Bill Bryden, the director, that there needed to be some suggestion early on of the epic nature of this story. It lay in that poem printed in the front of the book. Once I realised that it gave a truly epic ring to the story and would carry us through the quiet opening at the enquiry into the action that comes all too soon, I felt the work was truly on its way. We know by the end of the first minute that the ship is in disgrace, that its crew is mutinous, and that at least one senior admiral is anxious to inflict a terrible punishment on the crew and the ship. He sends them back to their doom...

ULYSSES: (VOICE OF SHIP)   Come my friends,
                  Tis not too late to seek a newer world.
                  To sail beyond the sunset, and the paths
                  Of all the western stars, until I die.
                  It may be that the gulfs will wash us down:
                  It may be we shall touch the Happy Isles,
                  And see the great Achilles, whom we knew
                                      that which we are, we are;
                  One equal temper of heroic hearts,
                  Made weak by time and fate, but strong in will
                  To strive, to seek, to find, and not to yield.

                              ★★★

THE WIND STOPS ITS INCESSANT WHINING AND THRUMMING. WE PICK UP THE SOFT TAP TAP OF A STICK IN THE LARGE OPEN WELL OF A WHITEHALL BUILDING. THE PACE IS DELIBERATE.

NICHOLLS: Assistant Director of Naval Operations Vice
                  Admiral Starr had a word for it. But then he
                  always did have.
STARR: Mutiny, gentlemen is the generally accepted
                  word for it. A capital offence. Commissioned
                  officers in His Majesty's Navy, including a flag
                  officer, sympathising with mutiny. You'd call it
                  something else perhaps. This?

In my script for *Dorian Gray*, which was adapted from a story by Oscar Wilde, there were a number of problems inherent in the story. Wilde's style has the overblown texture of an orchid: a colour, shape and perfume that are almost too rich a brew. Overblown too is the way in which Wilde tells his stories.

Gordon House, who directed the piece, and I, felt that we had to find a way to let this style be a part of the piece. This time, the solution was a more traditional one. The narrative line would be taken, in the first half, by the friend who leads young Dorian towards his decadence. The second half would use Dorian himself as the narrator who would lead the listener into the vile but tragic mind of this truly decadent protagonist.

> THE SOUND OF A SOIREE. A SCHUBERT DUET IS BEING PLAYED. THERE WILL BE A FLUTTER OF APPLAUSE FROM THE SMALL PARTY AS IT ENDS AND FADES. OVER IT LORD HENRY SPEAKS TO US. IT IS VERY COMPLICIT.

> LORD HENRY: Schubert, played by a girl in an exquisite dress. Candles and chandeliers sparkling in her hair and eyes. Art. Surface of course but art is all surface and symbol at once. Those who go beneath the surface do so at their peril. You remember Basil Hallward? The painter whose disappearance some years ago caused such public excitement and conjecture. He it was who painted the picture in question. My aunt had the young man in tow for some charity work.

> LEAK UP THE SCHUBERT
> ★★★

> LET MUSIC FADE TO ANOTHER ACOUSTIC AS WE FIND SIR HENRY AGAIN.

> LORD HENRY: I was in the habit of visiting Basil's studio regularly. It was summer and the studio was filled with the rich odour of roses. When summer breeze stirred the trees of the garden there came through the open door the heavy scent of lilac or the delicate perfume of the pink flowering thorn.

> BASIL: Well Henry, what d'you think of it?

Lord Henry's opening speeches gives us the sense of beauty, the Wildean *bon mot*, and a hint about a painter who died mysteriously: the hook, perhaps. Ian MacDiarmid played Sir Henry with deadly precision. The scene then develops, and by the end of the first minute we have had the first of the witty Wildean images which litter the whole story and which are, of course, a delight for any actor to use.

To look at something entirely different, the Western on radio is a daunting thing to attempt. All horses, cattle and guns, round-ups and shootouts, isn't it? And surely physical action isn't easy on radio? It isn't. But *Shane* is unusual in that the actual action is confined to cutting out the roots of a huge tree, riding into town on a buggy or a horse, and finally one shootout.

The shootout was going to provide problems, so I tried right at the beginning to prepare for that moment.

> THIS IS A MAN OF MATURE YEARS REMEMBERING IN TRANQUILLITY A PAST LIFE, PAST TIMES AND ONE EVENT THAT HAS BEEN A PIVOT OF HIS BELIEFS AND THE TOUCHSTONE OF HIS OWN WAY OF LIVING SINCE THE MOMENT SHANE RODE INTO TOWN.
>
> MUSIC: BANJO BEING PLUCKED SOFTLY.
> HEAR AT A LONG DISTANCE THE SOFT THUD OF A SLOWLY BEATING HEART. THIS WILL BE A RECURRING IMAGE BUT FOR THE MOMENT LET IT BE ON THE EDGES OF PERCEPTION. AS ROBERT MACPHERSON STARRETT, A MAN OF 64 REMEMBERS SLOWLY EASE IN THE CLATTER AND SOFT HOOF FALLS OF A LARGE HORSE ON A SUN BAKED COUNTRY ROAD AS IT MOVES SLOWLY THROUGH THE LAND TOWARDS THE RIVER.
>
> THE MEWING OF A HUNTING BUZZARD SOUNDS HIGH IN THE SKY. THE DISTANT SOUND OF WOOD BEING SAWED. COUNTRY SOUNDS OF CATTLE ALSO AT A DISTANCE. BUT THAT HEARTBEAT COMES CLOSER AND A TOUCH LOUDER AS IT DOES SO. FOR SHANE IS A HEARTBEAT AWAY IN THE MIND OF BOB STARRETT WHO IS TELLING THE STORY.
>
> (ROBERT WILL BE THE OLD MAN. BOB WILL BE THE BOY HE USED TO BE.)
>
> ROBERT: *He rode into our valley in the summer of '89. I saw him plain through that clear Wyoming air... Come through the cluster of the frame buildings that was our town,*

THE HOOFBEATS AND THE HEARTBEAT COME
INEXORABLY CLOSER

ROBERT: *Two cowhands on the open range side of the river looked up
as he rode past. They looked away and then stared after him.
He rode on, took the right fork away from the ford and Luke
Fletcher's big spread.*

I gave the directions in more detail than I usually do for two
reasons: one, I just felt the need to; and two, the show was being made
in America with American actors more used to TV than radio, and I
felt they'd need to have something to peg their performances to. I need
not have worried as it turned out.

The almost subliminal heartbeat sets up a tension in the listener and
will be something to use later on. This, the regular hoof-beats, and the
thudding of an axe into a tree are all there at this early stage to provide
that feeling of tension, of something about to happen. And all that is
happening is that Shane, a gunman who had hung up his guns, is riding
into the life of a young boy who is now an old man remembering.

It's a gentle, delicate opening for a Western. Edgy perhaps. It also
gives the listener a sense of where we are and the sort of community
this man is riding into. And they know – as Bob, the young boy, does
not – that this stranger riding into the community is a coiled spring...
and dangerous.

The effects were just touched in. There was nothing heavy-handed
in the production, which was directed by Anthony Cornish. I think this
is one of my favourite openings. The old man remembering being the
boy through whom the story of *Shane* is seen was Howard Keel.

So, let us recap on 'heads'. The opening has to hook the audience,
who might want to make tea, clinch an order on the phone, collect the
kids from school, set up the ironing board... But it also must set the
place, set the hero, set the style and the grammar. And it must give the
feeling that the listener is going to be in the hands of a real storyteller.

Tails – endings – are something else.

I have already remarked on the popularly quoted line from *A Tale of
Two Cities* spoken by the reckless, indolent, put-upon Sydney Carton
when the guillotine is about to fall. It only works if we truly believe him
and care for him when he claims that, 'It is a far, far better thing that I
do now than I have ever done before'. If we don't believe it, and if, by

the time we have got to this point, we do not care for him rather more than perhaps he deserves, it will not be anything but risible.

In this case, due to a fine performance from Charles Dance, we could and did believe. And after these words, the final revelations about the hero and heroine living happily ever after are almost unnecessary. Dickens has taken us on a journey with Carton, from dislike to love and with such understated skill that the translation to radio worked because the original writer made it easy to suspend disbelief and for the scene to work.

For really dramatic endings, like that of *HMS Ulysses*, a number of strands come together.

> THE WIND BEGINS TO KEEN AND WHINE AND GROW AS WE HEAR.

> ULYSSES:Ulysses, born along the Clyde by the towering forest of cranes, the thundering hammers, the arcing intense blue lights of welders and riveters, fitted with four Parsons turbines. A legend as a light cruiser, grown old on the Russian convoys. Her mission – locate, engage, destroy and now her turn. She died... died when the stars went out; died under the lash of her engines and the thrust of four vast screws... died in that whining wind off the Arctic wastes. Wind that cut flesh at 100 below. Died plunging into swelling black water that killed a man in three minutes if he was unfortunate to live that long... Died on that terrible Murmansk run... died in the tipped waves. Died on the Arctic circle at 40 degrees east. Beyond Bear Island. Died a legend. H.M.S. Ulysses.

The Admiralty enquiry into the loss of the mutinous ship has been both the top and the tail of the dramatisation. Nicholls, the one survivor, tries to explain to the old naval diehards how heroic the crew and the ship had been. They are more intent on saving their faces. The enquiry has been going on its quiet, ordered way, as Nicholls tries to put across to these older, traditional men the wonder of the end of the ship. We know what he is trying to say, because we have been there at sea, dying, being shot at, injured, angry and desperate with all the crew. But in this quiet room Nicholls is failing to get across the truth of the heroism.

Suddenly the voice of the ship itself cuts into the quiet, and we are there in the midst of the terrible fury that was her end. And after the sound and fury of that description, the sadness of the survivor tap tapping his way out of the enquiry gives a terribly sad coda to the whole epic story. And then, finally, the voice of Ulysses, quoting the Tennyson we'd heard at the opening of the play. It comes full and quiet circle.

In *The Strange Case Of Dr Jekyll And Mr Hyde* there is always looming the difficulty of that final transformation. In previous adaptations for film and stage, the audience had already been aware that Hyde was Jekyll and Jekyll was Hyde: one and the same person, with two personalities. In this version, we held back that knowledge until the very end.

It is always hard to write something that needs to be visual for a medium that is only sound; and with *The Strange Case Of Dr Jekyll And Mr Hyde* I was worried that the bits of broken dialogue and the overlapping speeches would just become rather embarrassing. I felt that I hadn't been able to crack the problem. But Nigel Anthony made the transformation work, in a *tour de force* of acting. Intercut with the words of a friend trying to help him, Jekyll, or is it Hyde, describes what it felt like to become viler and viler and to know that he was entirely out of control. That terrible moment when Jekyll realised that he no longer needed to take the liquid to become Hyde: it could happen to him overnight in bed. He tries to explain to the one friend who might understand.

The detail of the terror and of the exaltation of it, the revelling in evil and the revulsion from it, pour out of the two sides of the same man, overlapping and shifting from one to the other in a piece that is technically difficult for an actor. Nigel Anthony made it seem simple.

JEKYLL: DON'T... don't pity me. I will never reject that other half... that purely evil half for I am that man... I live through him. The evil I do... I revel in.

LANYON: Stop... I beg you to stop... Please.

JEKYLL: I tried to stop taking the potion and yet he forced himself through... always... I wanted to be Jekyll surrounded by friends. Good cheer and decency... I wanted more to be what I found in me and what now refuses to let me go. When my devil comes out now he comes in rage Lanyon. Roaring. I write blasphemies in books my father gave me... (HE IS SOBBING) If I go out I attack... A woman offered me a light... I

cut her... a child showed me her doll... I kicked her
face... a young man offered me a hand across the street
and I battered him to a pulp with my cane... I took
larger and larger doses of the chemical until I had
almost none left... Now...You have brought me the last.
What shall I do Lanyon... what can I do? I am
trapped... what can I do. What ever I do now... He will
come for me and there will be no return. None.

LANYON: (WRITING) So now you know what I knew my dear
Utterson. This friend of ours... Jekyll... Henry...
Hunted in every corner of the land in another form.
For the murder of our friend Carew, for abominable
things done... In the body of that concentrated evil...
Hyde... I dare not sleep... my dear friend. I dare not
sleep.

It's all there in the original story by Robert Louis Stevenson, and all
it needs is to dare to go for broke, as the actor did, and as I hope the
script helped him to do. No point in rewriting or looking for another
angle. The terror is all there in the original

Action, violent action, is always a concern for a radio dramatist, as
so often violence depends for its effect and power on the visual. If you
have set up a grammar which allows you to use a narrator, an outside
voice or the inside of a character's head, then it begins to be possible
to make violent action work. Maybe in radio the voices have to be
written with more bravura than would be necessary for film or
television. But then we come to the gunfight in *Shane*.

ROBERT: (OVER THE SOUND OF A MAN CRASHING
BACK AND THEN FORWARD OVER A BALCONY
AND SPLINTERING WOOD AND FINALLY
HITTING THE FLOOR. ALL IN SLOMO). *Stark
Wilson had cleared his holster when Shane's bullet took him
in the chest and a second shot from Shane finished him. But
Wilson had got one shot away before he died. Then Fletcher
shot at Shane from a balcony where he'd been hiding and
missed. I swear I never saw such grace as Shane flowed
across the room, getting his head forward, his legs set and the
barrel lined up like a finger pointing and flame... on an
instant and Fletcher crashed through the balcony floor.*

AND HEAR THE SOUND OF THE SPINNING CHAMBER OF
THE REVOLVER AS SHANE RELOADS IT AND THE

SILENCE ALL ROUND HIM. A GLASS FALLS AND BREAKS.

SHANE: I guess that about finishes it. I'll be riding now. And there's not one of you will follow.

ROBERT: *He turned his back on them and walked out of the of the saloon and not one of them moved. There was blood where he'd been hit by Wilson spreading over his chest but he walked out to his horse. He seemed overcome with weariness but his hands were steady. His strength still flowed, power surged up in the man.*

SHANE: Not one of you will follow...

BOB: (RUSHING TO HIM) Shane... Shane...

The fact that the FX have been so low-key in *Shane*, and that the storyteller, seeing again the action remembered, allows himself to become almost poetic in his retelling of it: lets the actual moment of the shoot-out become an audio version of slow motion. Only now the gunshots are very loud indeed! Then silence and the old man's voice tells quietly what he saw and still sees after all those years. And, in those words, we learn something of the sorrow a real gunman carried all his days. The goodbyes and the going away again are a coda only. The story has already been ended the minute Shane pulled the trigger on his enemy.

This is what radio does so well. It places writer and audience inside the heads of the protagonists and offers the writer the chance to probe and explore in a way that only novelists and radio writers are able to do.

Much of the skill of adaptation is trusting the original work to offer solutions to the problems as they emerge. Once actors and directors start to turn to the original text and to look for changes, new lines, different angles, you are dead in the water. So you have to provide a script which they too can believe is written as the original writer would have written radio if he had wanted to.

I suppose the real skill involved in dramatising for radio, apart from the necessity to work in the way I have described above, is to pick stories that you enjoy retelling. I have done two or three dramatisations which were hard, hard graft and it has always been because at heart I wasn't in love with the original story. On the other hand, take the end of *The Water Gypsies*. After writing TV cop shows, hospital dramas and the usual diet that television offers, what a relief to be able to confect something as gentle, guileless and decent as the five or six hours of radio that this was. Old fashioned and romantic and very warm. Here is Jane again – we first met her at the top of this piece – at the end of her story. It really did seem to write itself, and the story had gone full circle, which has a certain elegance to it.

JANE: (TO US) In the light of the old gas lamps I could see him standing there. So dependable, not a lot of romance maybe, warm, kindly... loving. (TO HIM) Hello Fred.

THE CRUNCH OF THEIR FEET AS THEY WALK SLOWLY TOGETHER ON GRAVEL.

FRED: (GENTLY) No need to say anything girl.
JANE: Bit tired of everything that's the truth. Everything sort of going wrong.
FRED: Muddle, that's all. It'll come right, you'll see. I thought mebbe we could take the dinghy out tomorrow. You could show me how well she sails.
HEAR THE DISTANT HOOTER OF BARGES
    If you'd like.
JANE: (GRABBING A LIFELINE) Fred... Yeah... Yes. Yes please.
AND THE MUSIC SWELLS TO THE END.

'Begin at the beginning, go on to the end, and then stop.'

FLYWHEEL, SHYSTER AND ME
Mark Brisenden

You can blame it on my dad I suppose. Why not? He used to blame everything on me when I was a child. And I mean everything. I had my pocket money stopped during the Cuban missile crisis. He didn't talk to me for a month after the assassination of Kennedy, just because I said I was at the library at the time. Well I could hardly admit to playing on the grassy knoll I wasn't allowed to go near. Instead he found other uses for me, the primary one being that every time a Marx Brothers movie came on the television I was parked in front of it with instructions to call him when Chico came on and started playing the piano. You must remember that this was in the mid-sixties, before video meant you could fast forward the love interest and Harpo's solo. Still, you've got to do something with children, and I'm sure Social Services only ever made a fuss about it because they were closet Abbott and Costello fans. Think about it though, what six-year-old wouldn't be entranced by Harpo's antics: the funny man with the odd walk and painted on moustache and the one with the pointy hat and an Italian accent worse than the current Pope's? These days all children have is playstations and cartoon channels. I feel so sorry for them.

Cut to twenty or so years later, and I'm reading the inestimable Dick Vosburgh's article in Punch magazine – well somebody had to buy it – about a book of rediscovered Marx Brothers radio scripts entitled *Flywheel, Shyster and Flywheel*. The rest, as they say, is geography. I bought the first copy I saw, read it faster than Jeffrey Archer can arrange an alibi, and then, alone and unaided, set out to cross Oxford Circus in the rush hour. News of my arrival at the BBC spread like wildfire and immediately set off the sprinkler system. Given that there were no known original recordings of these shows, I felt that if we could find actors good enough to recreate Groucho and Chico we would have a hit and a lot of fun on our hands. From there I was able to adapt and write enough original material to make eighteen shows. These went on to be nominated for several awards and actually win a Gold Medal at the International Radio Festival of New York. I know this because the BBC Producer I took the idea to very kindly gave me a photo of it.

My first moves into writing radio comedy had come several years earlier when, despairing of getting on to *Weekending* or *The News Huddlines*, I went along to a fringe theatre outfit called Newsrevue. To my delight, they started taking almost everything I could write. Not coming from a university background, I found the idea of four or five people performing sketches in a late night revue daring and original and wondered how long it had been going on. I wasn't found out until I had to ask one of the actors what he meant when he said one of my sketches was almost Brechtian in its approach. I was just hoping it was funny.

The break came when a local radio station, LBC, wanted us to broadcast a fifteen minute topical satire show every Monday evening for the princely sum of virtually nothing. Being the only writer not in other employment, I got the job as script editor and, on the day, re-write man. In the cast were two young impressionists, Rory Bremner and Jessica Martin. Rory was particularly handy, not just for his superb impressions, but for the fact that LBC was just down the road from the university he had attended. Turning up there mid-morning on a Monday, Rory would distract the attention of the Security Guard at the front desk while the cast and I would stroll in nice and casual and look as if we knew where we were going. Straight to the common room for free rehearsal space whilst the students were wasting their time attending lectures. In other words, don't let anybody tell you you need to have gone to the right university to write comedy – you just have to know how to sneak into them.

Nineteen eighty-four to -five was a good time to be writing comedy as the first wave of post-*Young Ones* writers and performers were beginning to happen in the pubs and clubs of London. I was heavily involved in one of these in Shepherds Bush when a stand-up comic and writer called Nick Revell told me that the BBC radio show *Weekending* had an open meeting for non-commissioned writers on Wednesday lunchtimes. I attended the very next one and they haven't been able to get rid of me since. I merely went up to the reception desk in the old BBC Light Entertainment department, announced I was there for the *Weekending* meeting and, once inside, got myself a Freelance Employee pass. I was in and, more importantly, I could use the subsidised canteen.

I owe my first BBC Radio 2 credit to Frank Sinatra. I'm not sure whether he ever realised this, and now I guess he never will. It came about like this. I was attempting, with my friend and then co-writer, Simon Bullivant, to do monologue items and quickies for the *News Huddlines* when we read that Sinatra had been injected with lamb's serum to increase the number of red blood corpuscles or some such nonsense. Getting the gag, but feeling it would be better performed first rather than written straight down, we went into the producer's lair and asked to do this. I then spoke the set-up about the Lamb's serum and added the punch, 'He's still the same man, but from now on he'll be doing everything (Baahing) Maaaaaaa Way'. I told you it didn't look good written down. This didn't prevent it getting broadcast, and I think we even stole some extra stationery supplies that day to celebrate.

My first line on *Weekending* I owe to Cliff Richard. If I haven't exactly worked with all the greats, I've certainly made sure to include them in my material. Back in the mid eighties, the show was still being recorded at the old Paris Studios and a collection of – I think the collective noun then was a 'moan' of – non-commissioned writers would huddle over the Friday morning papers and turn out news lines for what was then known as the 'next week's news' section of the show and for what is still known as pittance money. It gave a lot of us a toe-hold on the show and the opportunity to eat more than once a day. My first successful effort went something like this: 'Plans are announced to replace ancient national monuments such as Stonehenge with plastic replicas after the success of a similar experiment with Cliff Richard'.

Come on! Don't tell me you didn't know that that wasn't the real Cliff Richard. I was never able to be consistent enough to gain a commission first time around, but after a two-year disaster-strewn hiatus working in cabaret and learning that I wasn't really cut out to be a stand-up comedian, I returned for another crack at the small time. This time, I made it after a couple of months, getting commissioned on *Weekending* along with my friend, Simon Bullivant. At that time *Weekending* was a great job for those not independently wealthy or too paranoid to sign on and work. It ran about forty-two weeks of the year, and we got our jokes out of the papers from all the ridiculous things politicians, statesman and assorted dictators spent their waking hours doing. The brief of the show was simply 'a look back at the last seven days'. At that point in world affairs, this often involved the antics of Thatcher, Reagan, Heseltine, that week's Soviet leader and other well known despots. All you had to do was read the papers, successfully pitch for the story in the verbal blood-baths that passed for writers' meetings, and you had the first crack at writing the sketch. If you failed, never mind, there would be somebody right behind you just waiting to take over. In the end, I think I did about a nine-month stint, and I left primarily because in 1989 I became one of BBC Light Entertainment's contract writers – a grand-sounding title which effectively guaranteed me a certain amount a week or a year, regardless of what I got broadcast and which, when I added everything up at the end of the year, amounted to a pay cut. I've never been too good at the business side.

It was at about this time that I stumbled onto the published scripts of *Flywheel, Shyster and Flywheel*. Discovered by a researcher in the Library of Congress, the scripts were largely written by Nat Perrin and Arthur Sheekman, who were responsible for some of the best routines in *Duck Soup* and life-long friends of Groucho's. At first, I thought presenting these scripts would represent little work, and the joy, having been a life-long Marx Brothers fan, would just be in seeing them re-performed. Once we had had a first read through, including two superb performances of Groucho and Chico from actors recommended again by Dick Vosburgh, the script, minus sponsors' announcements, band orchestrations and guest singers, ran to a little under seventeen minutes. Well below that required for a modern radio half-hour.

From then on I adopted a process of weeding out the strongest material from the individual scripts, and bringing in good routines from scripts that otherwise were a little weak. It was quite a cut-and-paste job, along with the writing of the links and original material, to make up the half hours, and I'm grateful to my first ever word processor for making the job easier and sparing me an awful lot of re-typing. This worked fine until the end of the second series, when I was asked by the then head of Radio Light Entertainment if there was enough for a third. What else could I say but 'Yes', knowing full well there wasn't.

In the end, I wrote well over half the third series myself, and as a strict labour-of-love job this will never be surpassed until I can find those unrecorded W.C. Fields radio scripts. But don't worry, if I ever find any unrecorded Ritz Brothers material, I promise I'll leave it right where it is. What also made the job easier was that I had been a student of that period of American history for half my life, and, to my amazement, I realised that I understood most of the topical gags. Just for the sheer hell of it, I left one in a script during the second series. It went down as well as you can imagine a topical reference from nineteen thirty-three going down. The chief joy of the whole experience though, came from striking up a personal correspondence with, and finally meeting, one of the original writers, Nat Perrin. In his mid-eighties, but still writing, Nat was incredibly generous with his praise for all involved with the BBC versions. His assessment of my work on his and Arthur Sheekman's scripts was to call them, in one of his letters to me, my 'modestly termed adaptations'. I know I will never get higher praise in my career for anything! Having Spike Milligan and Dick Vosburgh appear in two episodes in the third series was also a career high.

For the last six or seven years, amongst other things, I have been one of the regular commissioned writers on *The News Huddlines*, the Roy Hudd-fronted topical comedy show. Now that *Weekending* has gone and still not been fully replaced with a regular weekly show that accepts outside submissions, *The Huddlines* remains the best bet for a non-commissioned writer to send stuff to. The main difference between this and the old *Weekending* is that *The Huddline*s is recorded in front of a live and sometimes fully awake audience, and they expect the show to make them laugh. Hardly grateful considering they get their tickets free. Nobody said life or comedy was fair.

If you wish to attempt to write for the show this is how I suggest you go about it. First and extremely foremost, and I can't write this loud enough... LISTEN TO THE SHOW BEFORE YOU SUBMIT ANY MATERIAL TO IT. That rule goes for any show you are thinking of writing for, even if it only means you find out the producer's name. Producers are funny that way. They like it when you use their name and not the name of the person who was doing it seven years ago. Having been a writer on the show for quite some time, I can also guarantee that every line, every sketch and every quickie submitted gets read by at least the script editor and the compiler of the weekly opening monologue. However, if the first line of your sketch involves a much loved children's television character or a member of the Royal Family involved in deviant sexual practices, it is doubtful whether the second line will be read and, if it is, it is probably only out of the script editor's morbid curiosity concerning the state of your mental health or his desire to try the practice for himself... Hey, you don't know our script editor!

First let me tell you what not to write. If you listen to the show – and you damn well better had now – you'll notice its overall structure. Sometimes there is an up-to-the-minute topical quickie before the opening credits. This is usually written on the morning of the recording, so I wouldn't bother with it. This is followed by the monologue – a twenty to thirty-gag opening based around the week's news, serious and silly. Of which more in a minute. The monologue is often followed by a political sketch of the week focusing either on Blair or Howard or sometimes both. This is always written by the same writer, and a very good one at that, so it's only worth submitting quickies or incidental stuff around the major political events. Same goes for the royal sketches: they have been written by the same writer for a long time and he shows no sign of slowing down or running out of good, funny material.

This also holds true for the songs: they are all specially commissioned along with the pastiche Billy Bennett boom-boom monologues the show sometimes uses. The writer of these is uncanny and he can do them until the cows come home. How he finds the time with the milking and the mucking out and driving to market I do not know. If you think I'm just trying to put you off and protect our work, let me tell you that I myself do none of the above. But, if you want to have a go, nothing is stopping you. I am just trying to maximise your chances of getting something on the show. So what does that leave you? Everything else. First, there is the monologue. This is a great way to break into the show. It consists almost entirely of non-commissioned material faxed, e-mailed and sent in from all over. Start hitting regularly and your name will be noticed and you might even get a line commission which can then lead you onto the sketch writing side of things. Two things about monologue items. Bizarre as some of them may sound, all the stories are true and taken from that week's papers.

Even the ones involving superglue, wedding tackle and a household appliance in the same sentence. Second, keep them short. A one-liner is not called that because it's a paragraph and a half long. Here are a couple of examples of my own:

> 1. ROY   And did you see that when Al Fayed dies he wants to be embalmed, mummified and displayed in a glass case on top of Harrods? Good idea, let's do it tomorrow.

> 2. ROY   And did you read about the man who did a university course on the seventies cop series, The Sweeney? Yes, they didn't give him a degree, they just threw the book at him.

You get the picture? One sentence set up outlining the story. Second sentence punchline. And I don't want to see you doing it any differently.

Alternatively, you might like to try your hand at quickies. Again, as the name suggests, these don't last very long. Half a page ideally, but certainly no more than a page, and it had better have a damn funny punchline. This can be on almost any subject taken from any of the papers – within the bounds of taste, of course, so best to avoid serial killers and child prostitution – just so long as you set the story up so that the audience can follow and know why they're laughing at the punchline. Below is an example I had broadcast, with added notes. Remember: apart from the studio audience everybody else only gets to hear the show, so make good use of sound effects and sometimes music, though for *The Huddlines* most of that is provided by the house band taking a day off from their Salvation Army work.

LOVER'S FAST LANE

> 1. GRAMS.   'JUST ONE CORNETTO'. OUT.
>   (ALL OF A SUDDEN WE ARE IN ITALY)
> 2. FX.   TRAFFIC ATMOS. UNDER (AND IN TRAFFIC NO LESS)
> 3. ROY   (SMOOTH ITALIAN) Ah, Bella Bella, my sweet Donatella, you make love like an angel.
> 4. JUNE   (ITALIAN) Isn't it wonderful that we can do this now.
> 5. CHRIS   (APPROACHING) Ay, Police. What do you think you do?
> 6. ROY   Ay, Officer. It's legal now for Italian couples to make love in the car, so long as the doors are locked.

4-6   (DIALOGUE THE GIST. STORY AND SETUP)
7. CHRIS   All right. I let you go this time. But next time,
           remember.
8. ROY   What?
9. CHRIS   Go when the light changes to green. (PULL BACK
           AND REVEAL PUNCHLINE)

Now, barring the subjects I warned you against above, there is
nothing to stop you writing sketches about any other topic suitable for
the *Huddlines* treatment from that week's news. Fire away. Write as
many as you want, but a word of warning here. The producer and the
script editor will be far more impressed by quality than quantity. It is far
better to send two really good sketches that you have spent time on and
are happy with than to rush off four and hope for the best. Also, do
spend time on your punchlines. Nothing disappoints a script editor
more than reading a fairly good or usable sketch that is let down by a
poor punchline. Sometimes it is possible to fix and put the sketch in the
script anyway; at other times there is just too much else to do and no
one ever quite gets round to it. If necessary spend as much time, or
more, on your punch as you have spent on the entire rest of the sketch.
It will pay off. Also, it doesn't always go that the punch line has to be
the funniest line of the sketch. It's great if you can do it, but what it most
needs to be is the best imaginable ending for the piece, even if it seems
too obvious sometimes. Even the great writer and director Billy Wilder
said, 'Let the audience add up two plus two. They'll love you forever'.
Do bear in mind though that even a sketch needs a cogent beginning,
middle and end, along with a little character development – no matter
how slight – and a fairly logical progression of events.

So that's just about it as far as *The Huddlines* goes, but the rule is the
same whatever the comedy radio programme. Listen or watch any
comedy show you want to contribute to first; get the producer's name;
and send your material off to them. The BBC Light Entertainment
department also has its own writers' guidelines, which you can obtain by
writing to the current producer of *The News Huddlines*. No, I'm not going
to tell you their name. You'll have to listen to the show. The most
important thing to remember is that most, if not all of the current crop of
commissioned writers, including me, came through the routes I have just
described. Now, what I want to know is how the hell you get off this show!

Writing for Radio and TV
Sue Teddern

Radio-drama. Like Bakewell tart and beach huts, it's something we Brits do better than any other country in the world. Those of us who grew up with it love it and would be lost without it, even though it can often irritate the hell out of us. But there's also a huge band of people who've never heard of it. Or have never heard it. They may well have to contract a serious illness and be confined to bed to discover the pleasures of a morning serial or afternoon play, once they've OD'd on *Neighbours* and *Ready Steady Cook*.

I was lucky. I grew up with radio-drama. There were special shows just for me and my mates, like *Listen with Mother*. I also remember coming home from school and listening with mother to *Mrs Dale's Diary*. When that was replaced by *Waggoner's Walk*, I listened to that too. But as a young adult, radio-drama disappeared from my life.

Funnily enough, it was moving to Amsterdam that brought it back; first as a listener, then as a writer. I was deputy editor of KLM's in-flight magazine and didn't own a TV. So I relied on Radio 4 and that's when I got hooked on *The Archers*. It was strangely surreal, listening to everyday stories of country folk as I watched a benign flock of junkies gambol past my canal house window. Ambridge kept me linked to a Britain that contrasted wildly with the news reports of Galtieri, Goose Green and the Gang of Four.

One of our magazines was produced for an airline which flew to Birmingham. So when the editor decided to run a feature about the world's longest-surviving soap, I lobbied to write it. It was glorious; I visited Pebble Mill and watched *The Archers* being recorded, met the actors and discovered the world behind the microphone. I was hooked and decided to have a go at it myself.

A sample *Archers* script got me a commission and that led to a second. It was even more surreal listening to my own episodes from that very Amsterdam canal house. When I moved back to England, I thought they'd snap me up. But my third batch of scripts didn't make the grade, and now I am less than a nano-blip in the history of *The Archers*... even though I did give Nigel Pargetter his very first speaking line. Inspired, I joined an evening class where I took forever to write *Sauce,* a radio play about a bumptious restaurant reviewer. A year later, a producer found it in an 'in' tray and, joy of joys, we cast the late Jack May (aka Nelson Gabriel) in the starring role. Encouraging reviews convinced me I wasn't wasting my time. I could do this.

An Arvon Foundation writing course was the next big milestone. It opened my eyes to the pleasures of writing for TV; those purely visual moments which don't need to be explained to the eager listener in the car, kitchen or bath. I seem to recall one of my tutors warning me that I might find it difficult writing for TV *and* radio. It hasn't caused me any problems but more of that later...

I wrote a few sub-standard sitcom scripts, thinking I could replicate the rubbish already on the screen. But they found me out, and that was a very useful lesson. I also wrote another radio play (which began life as a 15-minute film) *Remember This,* a romance set at an airport during an air traffic controllers' strike. Having it broadcast convinced me I wasn't a one-hit wonder.

It was *Remember This* which helped get me on to the *Birds of a Feather* team. Altogether I wrote 13 episodes and it was an invaluable apprenticeship; writing for TV, writing for existing characters; writing for a sitcom the nation took to its heart. The money was nice too. Since then, I've been paid handsomely to write endless treatments and pilot scripts for TV series. Some get closer to the winning post than others but it can be a dispiriting business.

And then, a few years ago, I returned to radio-drama, co-writing with Georgia Pritchett two series of linked plays, one based around the song *My Way* and the other with the theme of Mother's Day. This gave me the taste for both single plays and series. And that's where I am now!

For the last few years I've written for TV and Radio. So I'm probably in a good position to compare and contrast the two media. Which is better? And why? Which comes easier? And why? Which gives me the most satisfaction? And why?

Even as I list those questions, I don't know the answers. The structural techniques I've learnt don't vary, depending on whether my script is going to be seen or heard. But obviously, one must approach radio with the knowledge that everything must be described – the 'who, what and where' of each scene. In TV, a facial expression, shade of lipstick or time of day can be worth a thousand words. How do you do this on radio?

Below is a scene from *Lucky Heather*, a six-part comedy-drama which was broadcast on Radio 4 in February 2000, starring Lindsay Coulson. Heather lives on a down-at-heel housing estate, loves Westerns and has become, in her own words 'a cross between a private eye and a nosey parker'. In episode six, Heather is asked to follow her ex, Joe, in order to find out if he's cheating on his wife.

Following someone makes very poor radio. Obviously Heather doesn't want to advertise her presence, so how could I indicate where she is and what she's up to? In other episodes I opted for the good old mobile phone so that she could offer a kind of running commentary on her whereabouts. But in this scene, I wanted to establish the kind of place Joe would choose to meet his latest girlfriend. That's where the waiter, comes in:

INT. BUSY DOME-TYPE CAFE. HEATHER SITS AT A REAR TABLE. 'LA FEMME D'ARGENT' BY AIR IN THE BACKGROUND.

WAITER	Can I get you another coffee?
HEATHER	I'm up to here with caffeine.
WAITER	We do a brilliant pear tart. I had three slices yesterday.
HEATHER	Okay, I'll have a decaff latte and some pear tart. It's only fruit, isn't it.
WAITER	And why not move to a table by the window? Nobody can see you here.
HEATHER	I'm fine.
WAITER	I'd bring a book next time. 'Penguin Modern Classics' always go down well.
HEATHER	Sorry?
WAITER	Makes you look intellectual. *City Listings* magazine said this is the fifth best place in town to 'meet' people. I see it happening all the time.
HEATHER	I can see it happening right now.

WAITER	Anyone you've got your eye on? I could go up to them and say: the lady by the salad bar wonders if you'd care to join her.
HEATHER	That man near the window. With the blonde.
WAITER	Forget it. Love's young dream, we call those two. You can do better than him. What about that chap with the glasses?
HEATHER	Do they come here a lot?
WAITER	Couple of times a week. Can't keep their hands off each other. (BEAT) Oh God, you're not his wife, are you?
HEATHER	Don't worry. The only aisle we walked down was Tesco's. Ooh, she's going. I might have a quick word. (DEP)

Without wanting to pick this scene to pieces, it's worth analysing it in a little more detail to see how I opted to feed in all the relevant information. The listener needs clues as to where we are. But it mustn't be too clunky and obvious.

So... first of all, don't be afraid to use background music. It can instantly colour-in a scene without intruding. In this case, I chose a very distinctive, instrumental track to imply a chi-chi bistro. Talk of 'decaff latte' and 'pear tart' also establishes that this is not a greasy spoon, snack bar or pub.

'I'm up to here with caffeine' is a line that could work on TV or radio. It subtly informs the listener that Heather has been sitting here for quite a while and works far better than 'I've been sitting here for quite a while'! The section about the cafe being an upmarket pick-up joint might also imply that Joe's no stranger to the place or to meeting young women there. Some of the waiter's other lines reveal that this couple are in the early stages of their relationship and are so wrapped up in each other that the staff have begun to notice them. If this was a TV scene, I could dispense with dialogue altogether. Here goes:

INT: CAFE-AFTERNOON
This is a trendy Dome-style cafe where single-but-searching people come to linger over carrot cake and cappucino. *HEATHER* sits at a table near the back, cleverly screened from *JOE* behind the salad bar. From her POV; we see *JOE* and *KATH* holding hands, kissing, practically all over each other. The WAITER approaches *HEATHER*, empties several cigarette ends from her ash tray and

removes her empty coffee cup and cake plate. He says something to her; *HEATHER* studies the menu, shakes her head and wearily lights another fag. Suddenly *KATH* stands, kisses *JOE* goodbye and exits. *HEATHER* stubs her cigarette out and approaches *JOE*.

Both work in their own way. 'I'm up to here with caffeine' has been replaced by the full ash tray – which obviously only works if your character smokes! In the TV version, the waiter isn't required to have any kind of personality. In fact, he isn't required at all. But the glorious thing about radio is that an actor is hired to breathe life into a minor character who is really only there for information purposes. In this case, actor David Holt, gave the waiter a wonderfully camp Kenneth Williams tone and was very funny. You have to keep cast numbers down but there's no reason why the same actor can't also play one or two other minor parts. On radio, you can do that!

It's actually a very useful exercise, comparing and contrasting TV and radio. Some radio successes, like *Spoonface Steinberg*, *After Henry* and *People Like Us*, have famously made the transition from aural to visual. Lee Hall's moving monologue about a dying child was pure radio. You lived inside the head of Spoonface and didn't need to see her world to understand it. Simon Brett's *After Henry* worked well in its TV format. But personally I feel it lost some of the intimacy its radio predecessor offered. And it changed from a comedy-drama to a sitcom, which required more laughs-per-page than the radio series. And a studio audience! As for *People Like Us*, by John Morton, both versions were brilliant. Out went some of the word-play gags, in came a wonderful array of visual ones.

But I can't help thinking that these three creations began on radio for a reason. And not just because the commissioning process is less prescriptive and safe. Radio-drama can be more claustrophobic, more cerebral, more evocative, more atmospheric.

I've been in countless radio studios, watched all manner of actors – young, old, fat, thin, scruffy, smart – pretend to be someone else, somewhere else. And even though I wrote the words and saw them recorded, as soon as I hear the finished play, I'm instantly transported to the cow shed, *palais de danse* or homeless hostel. The cliché about the pictures being better on radio couldn't be more true!

Television eats up ideas. If they're long-running hits like *Casualty*, even better. And if you're the writer who created the format, you will be one very happy (and wealthy) bunny. But unless you're lucky enough to get a screenplay commission, there are no slots for single plays or one-offs. *Clocking Off* is as close as it gets. People hark back to the good old days of *Play for Today* and *Armchair Theatre*. But those days are gone. So where do you place your single play? Radio, of course.

Another genre that radio embraces is period drama. I'm not saying TV fails this. Look at *Vanity Fair* and *Pride and Prejudice*. But period drama on TV doesn't come cheap. Apart from all the costumes, some poor soul has to search out the village which, with careful planning, can be transformed into 1920s Barnsley or 1820s Bath. Out go the speed bumps, phone boxes and Sock Shops. In come the penny farthings, street urchins and newspaper boys, invariably shouting: 'War declared. Read all about it!'

It's a costly business; perhaps that's why only the top echelon of writers – Andrew Davies, Adrian Hodges or Alan Bleasdale – are trusted with such projects. On radio, you can set your drama in the Crimea, the Coronation or the Cavern. No corsets or codpieces required. And if you like, you can still have that irritating newspaper boy doing his stuff.

I've written two series of a four-part radio-drama called *The Charm Factory*. It's set in early '50s London and tells the story of a group of up-and-coming film stars. Yes, I researched my socks off to evoke the era when meat was still rationed and frothy coffee was a novelty. But thanks to the magic of radio, the atmosphere kicks in from the start. A burst of newsreel, a blast of Alma Cogan, and you're there. It even sounds black-and-white!

I hoped the first series would transfer to television. A lovely review in *The Guardian* even predicted it would. But only Carlton – briefly – showed an interest. When I wrote series two, I forgot about its TV possibilities and let my imagination take over. So I have film premieres, gala parties, East End pubs, Soho jazz clubs, church fetes, trains, planes, cars, you name it. And a cast of thousands. I am God and I rule my post-war world.

I also feel that certain dramatic devices suit radio far better than television. Narration can work well in TV and there are plenty of successful examples to hold up as proof. But cynics might wonder if occasionally it's tacked on afterwards because the story didn't unfold clearly enough. When the narrator's description belies what we see on the screen, it can be a brilliant tool. But you can do that on radio too.

I've used narration several times. In my very first play, *Sauce*, there were two stories running in parallel. The narration took the form of the published restaurant review; full of pomposity and verbiage. Meanwhile, the play itself revealed the true events of the evening; the temporary secretary, brought along as the reviewer's companion, who was less than impressed with his cheesy chat-up lines. And the crises in the kitchen that the chef/owner had to cover up.

I also used an opening monologue by Heather at the beginning of each episode of *Lucky Heather* to set the scene for any new listeners. It was important each week to describe the estate she lived on, her passion for Westerns, her attitude to her community... and to establish the theme of each week's story. This is the opening monologue from episode four:

> HEATHER   I have these fantasies of being under the stars in Wyoming or wherever with my favourite cowboy. Sometimes it's James Stewart in *Destry Rides Again*. Sometimes it's Steve McQueen in *The Magnificent Seven*. More often than not it's Clint Eastwood in faded jeans. Shut your eyes and Clint'll haul you up on to the back of his Palomino and gallop you away from the tower blocks and tat of the Sutter Estate. Mind you, the Sutter can be very romantic at dusk, when the blossom's out and the wheely-bins are empty. We have our moments. Well, I don't. That's where Clint comes in! The thing about Clint is he isn't real. He's the man with no name. In my experience it's the men with names who give you grief. Bitter and twisted? Who me?

As I said earlier, radio casts can often double up. Those of us who know and love the genre will be extremely familiar with the announcer's line in the end-credits: 'Other parts were played by members of the cast'. I've worked with some incredible 'stars' over the years: Stephen Tompkinson, June Whitfield, Douglas Henshall, Dinah Sheridan, Anita Dobson... But the joy of radio-drama also comes from the huge band of versatile, talented, inventive actors who aren't always famous faces, often members of the RDC repertory company.

And although the clever sound-engineers can mock up the

background chit-chat of a crowded cocktail party or the hubbub of a busy airport, you can't write speaking parts for a cast of thousands. That may seem like a restriction but it's a healthy one. If you know you can only run to six speaking parts, you cut your cloth accordingly. And what seems like a handicap turns into a blessing... honestly!

I'm certainly not saying radio-drama is the only genre so forget about theatre, film and TV. Having just written two radio plays in quick succession, it was bliss to return to a TV script and be allowed to play with a whole new box of visual toys. Perhaps it's left brain/right brain work. And I like exercising both. And, it has to be said, telly pays better.

I've loved it in the past when someone has told me they enjoyed one of my episodes of *Birds of a Feather*. Watching television is definitely a shared experience. But when you meet someone who accidentally stumbled upon a radio play of yours and tells you they couldn't get out of their car until it was finished, that is true praise. A good radio play gets inside your head, and the experience is unique to you the listener alone. Listen to this afternoon's play – whatever it is – and see what I mean.

THE BALLAD OF CHARLES PARKER
Christopher Hawes

It begins with the driving train-rhythm of a blue-grass banjo strumming. Then the voice enters: Ewan McColl, unmistakably, the original finger-in-the-ear folk singer, composer of 'Dirty Old Town' and 'The First Time That Ever I Saw Your Face', a voice full of proletarian pride, a seamless, gritty Scots integrity.

> John Axon was a railwayman
> To steam trains born and bred
> He was an engine driver
> At Edgeley loco shed
> For forty years he followed
> And served the iron way
> He lost his life upon the track
> One February day...

Then, over the banjo strum, the announcer: a plummy BBC voice (you can almost see the dinner jacket) reads the official Ministry of Transport report of the accident:

> Ministry of Transport and Aviation, July 10th, 1957. Sir, I have the honour to report that, as a result of my enquiry into the collision that occurred on Saturday the 9th of February 1957, when the eleven five freight train from Buxton to Arkley got out of control as it was descending a deep incline on the down line, and overtook and collided violently with the rear of the eight forty five am freight train from Rowsley to Edgeley, I regret to report that driver Axon and the guard of the Rowsley freight train were killed...

The opening moments of 'The Ballad of John Axon', the first of the series of 'radio ballads' composed and produced by the team of McColl, his wife Peggy Seeger and the BBC Producer Charles Parker between the years 1957 to 1970. For years, they existed only in memory and a series of long-deleted LPs. Suddenly, last year, several were reissued by Topic Records on CD.

They sound rather old-fashioned nowadays. They belong to a time when interest in, and use of, regional, 'demotic' speech, or 'vox pop', must have been seen as exotic, daring, even revolutionary, and, above all, important. What was important about it all was high on the intellectual left-wing agenda; and there were plenty of 'those sort of young people' at the BBC, still heady with the post-war Labour victory and all the brash talk that had gone round about a Brave New World and a classless society. The nation was just emerging from the post-war years of austerity, rationing and general greyness. The Reithian BBC, prompted by the post-war new Labour (as opposed to New Labour) government, had embarked on the rather jolly mission to 'celebrate the ordinary'.

In other words, to cheer us all up about ourselves, radio producers were dispatched to the industrial north laden with tape machines to record the authentic voice of a proletariat that had, (with due leadership from the officer class, of course) done its damnedest and won the war. Mass Observation was continuing to conduct its sociological surveys of working-class life, a somewhat clinical exercise in which Oxbridge graduates found themselves skulking behind Blackpool sand dunes taking detailed notes on the mating behaviours of 'courting couples'. George Orwell had just published his essays on popular culture in *The Lion and the Unicorn*. Wilfred Pickles' popular *Have A Go* quiz game was touring the factory canteens, and the bucolic British music hall tradition, enjoying a post-war revival, was gratefully received into many middle class living rooms via the wireless and shows like *Happidrome* and *Variety Bandbox*.

> 'Have you got a bottle of red oil for a red tail-light?'
> 'Where've you been for it? Bloody Arabia?'

Parker and McColl created what amounted to a fresh radio art form. John Axon, a steam-train engine driver, had died in his cab because he stayed with his runaway train to try and warn the signal-man of the train he was rushing towards. The Ballad is an elegy to his name, eliding taped voices of John Axon's workmates, friends and family in his home town of Stockport, into McColl and Seeger's eclectic score, mixing traditional folk rhythms with jazz and calypso.

> You give her water, you give her coal
> Hand on the regulator, watch her roll,
> Mama, I swear, as long as I live
> Gonna serve the steam locomotive.
>
> Mama, listen to my narrative
> Gonna serve the steam locomotive...

Charles Parker had been excited by the wartime propaganda documentary films of Humphrey Jennings (*Speak for Britain*) and John Grierson, which celebrated the heroism of 'the man in the street'. He was one of the first (along with the likes of Olive Shapley) to take the speech of 'ordinary' (i.e. working class) people and use their eloquence as raw material for complicated, expensive and carefully wrought radio programmes.

It's a sort of documentary opera. The Ballads created a sensation, pulling in huge audiences, being exported to many foreign countries, and having an undoubted influence on the 'political' theatre of the rest of the fifties and sixties, most notably via Charles Chilton (another BBC Radio man) and Joan Littlewood's Theatre Workshop's *Oh, What A Lovely War!*

> What a feeling you have when you get up to strength! You've got the engine, you've got the control of it, and what a feeling. I'm cock of the bank. There's nobody can take a rise out of me now. She's mine. Come on, me old beauty, and off we go ...

'John Axon' and the seven further Ballads ('Singing the Fishing', 'The Big Hewer' *et al*) celebrated the harshness of the lives of miners, fishermen, railway men and so on. They undoubtedly idealised and iconised the 'working man', even taking a kind of macho pride in the hardships they endured. But 'John Axon' conveys above all the pleasure, even the poetry of the steam train era.

> Look at that moonlight, it's beautiful. There's nothing like the feeling of standing on the foot plate on a night like this...

Some of the most beautiful music is given to female voices, but women for the most part play secondary roles as girlfriends or mothers or wives.

> Jack and I were keen on rambling. That was how we met. I lived at Stretford. Jack lived at Stockport. Sometimes we went on moonlight rambles...

For the most part, they do so movingly: and some of the interviews with women are very strong; but they tend to be restricted to the roles of a chorus of mourners over the disasters depicted. And politically, the Ballads wear their hearts on their sleeves. Perhaps this is why they strike us quaintly in the twenty-first century, when overtly political statements (especially leftish ones), if not sufficiently post-modernised, are met with cynicism and disbelief. And when, as Peggy Seeger has said, 'People aren't used to just sitting and listening to radio any more'.

But when Axon's engine-driver neighbour says of the railway man's stock in trade, 'It was part of your life... Railways went through the back of your spine like Blackpool went through rock,' it's not over-sentimental, surely, to feel a sense of deep regret and loss. And to remember that in its day 'Singing the Fishing', about three generations of herring fishermen (and including the classic McColl song 'Shoals of herring') won the 1960 Prix Italia for radio documentary and was transmitted in 86 countries.

> 'With a steam locomotive, you create the power, you maintain the power, and you control the power...'

When you realise that it took three weeks to edit the 250 or so hours of tape amassed for each programme, the legends about Parker breaking into the BBC in order to work on them overnight begin to make sense.

The Ballads were all recorded live, with the tape machine in the same studio as the band, not mixed in later, the voices part of the overall music of the piece. No wonder that the BBC began to complain to Parker about 'making disproportionate demands upon resources'.

Then, in 1970, the accountants won the argument. The BBC was beginning to pursue ratings rather than more populist agendas, and the axe fell on the Radio Ballads. Or, perhaps, the concept had, like John Axon, simply run out of steam. When Parker was invited, instead, to apply his talents to making 10-minute inserts for *Woman's Hour*, he declined the offer, and was duly sacked. Outraged letters appeared in the newspapers. Questions were asked in the House of Commons.

> The run it is finished
> The shift's nearly ended,
> So long, mates, so long,
> Remember: a man is a man,
> And he must do what he can
> For his brothers,
> By his deeds you shall know him,
> By the work of his hands,
> By the friends who will mourn him,
> By the love that he bore,
> By the gift of his courage...

It's not hard to imagine how much of a stir the *Ballads* made in their day. To my ears they still come over as fresh, bold and moving, and essentially truthful, not, as they have been accused, stuck in the ideology of Soviet-era posters of happy tractor drivers and muscle-bound factory-workers.

This year, a group of Sheffield undergraduates studying radio-drama found 'John Axon' impossible to take seriously – too didactic, too slow, naive, even. One student called it 'patronising'. And yet in its day it was described by one radio critic as 'as remarkable a piece of radio as I have ever listened to'.

Of course, these days, 'vox pop' and 'actuality' have become staple radio (and television) fare. And fly-on-the-wall documentaries buzz around the nightly schedules to the point of self-parody. And today's radio-drama/documentarians are surely going to need to find new forms and new ideas that don't simply rely on rambling narratives or opinions recorded on street corners. Certainly, the technology available, the ability to mix, edit and sample in a matter of seconds, has made life much simpler for audio diarists and programme makers. No doubt, Charles Parker would have given his editing arm for access to such marvels. Or would he? I have a feeling that we would find him still sneaking into the BBC after dark to work through the night with tape reels, razor blade and editing block.

Parker, McColl and Seeger's legacy still seems to me a immensely rich one. As the industries they celebrate in the *Ballads* fade into the blue remembered hills of nostalgia, they give us more than just an authentic record of a disappearing way of life, but a celebration of pride, of community, too – Old Labour values all.

They still deserve to be listened to. When I came to write my radio play *The Snow Field* (broadcast on Radio 4 in 1993 and directed by Kate Rowland in Manchester), I drew to some extent on the post war BBC and its attempts to identify the 'working class experience'. Perhaps the story of my protagonist, Dorothy Headley, was not a million miles away from that of Charles Parker.

Dorothy Headley, a radio producer from London with her roots in the North, comes to work for the BBC in a city that could be Leeds or Sheffield. She discovers and encourages the writing of a young steelworker, George Leyburn. He is bursting with ideas and images, but arouses the resentment of his family and neighbours by cannibalising their lives for his stories. This is particularly hard for his wife, Ellie, on whom he plays the cruel trick that gives the play its title: taking her blindfolded up on to the moors after a snowstorm and turning her loose in the immense (and to Ellie terrifying) whiteness, nothingness. This becomes the central image of the play, the whiteness of the field standing partly as a metaphor for the white page that waits for the writer to make his mark upon it. And George's use of the incident in the first of his broadcast stories makes Ellie literally sick.

GEORGE   The girl was very frightened. Away from her familiar
            streets with their dark chimneys and frosted roofs,
            nothing could shield her from the deafening silence
            of the sky, the terrifying distances from star to star. It
            was a kind of test for her, all education he called it.
            He led her up, blindfolded, out of the safe sound of
            the cobbled streets into a muffled place, snow deep
            underfoot, the wash of trees in the wind, the hard,
            sharp, frost smack of the air. He pushed her, hard,
            out into the white world, into the snow field.
ELLIE   It's all... white... It's nothing, it's like there's nothing.
GEORGE   Like stepping off the edge of the world.
ELLIE   There's nothing, there's nothing, there's nothing.
GEORGE   Just look at it, girl, look at it.
ELLIE   I can't.
GEORGE   It's beautiful, is that. There's more to the world than
            streets and houses, girl.
ELLIE   There's nothing...

| GEORGE | Nothing there to hurt you, don't you see? |
| ELLIE | Nothing, nothing, nothing, (RISING TO A SCREAM) Nothing! Nothing! Nothing! |

Dorothy's first meeting with George, in the foyer of the Midland Hotel, gives the latter his first taste of the world he longs for, as far as he can possibly get from the terraced streets where he was born.

INT. THE LOBBY OF THE MIDLAND HOTEL.

GEORGE	Miss Headley.
DOROTHY	Mr Leyburn.
GEORGE	I knew it were you. I'm George Leyburn. I'm not late, am I?
DOROTHY	No, you're rather early.
GEORGE	I ran all t'way. I've just come off shift. I'm sorry about Ellie not telling me you came round.
DOROTHY	She was most insistent that you had your sleep.
GEORGE	She should have told me. I read your letter. Thanks. 'We are grateful to you for sending us your story. We think that it shows great promise.'
DOROTHY	You know the words by heart.
GEORGE	I've read them through that many times. Where's the other bloke, then?
DOROTHY	I beg your pardon?
GEORGE	'We are grateful'... 'We think'
DOROTHY	We have to use the formal 'we' in letters, I'm afraid. It's rather expected.
GEORGE	Who expects it?
DOROTHY	Our Lords and Masters at the BBC.
GEORGE	You could have written in bloody Chinese for all I cared. I'm sorry, Miss Headley. I think it's the best feeling I've ever had in my life.
DOROTHY	Well, then, I'm very glad.
GEORGE	And are you going to put it out, then, my story, on wireless?
DOROTHY	I've shown it to my boss. He's approved it. But we'll have to do some work on it first.
GEORGE	I'm sorry?
DOROTHY	Some revisions, some rewriting.
GEORGE	Oh.
DOROTHY	Don't look so crestfallen.
GEORGE	Revisions...
DOROTHY	It is usual.
GEORGE	I don't know what you mean.

DOROTHY	Well, we may have to trim a little.
GEORGE	Trim...
DOROTHY	For length.
GEORGE	But I thought you said you liked it.
DOROTHY	I do like it, very much.
GEORGE	You said so, you told me.
DOROTHY	Mr Leyburn, perhaps I'd better explain.
GEORGE	I don't understand.
DOROTHY	Well, first of all, there are time slots to consider.
GEORGE	Time slots? What are they?
DOROTHY	I'll explain. Say a programme is scheduled for nine thirty in the evening. Well, our listeners at home have a sort of contract with us, I like to think, and we have one with them, to broadcast a programme at exactly that time, and that means that material to be broadcast sometimes has to be... trimmed a little, to fit the time slots. Do you see?
GEORGE	And this 'material', what's that, then? Is that what my story is, then? 'Material'?
DOROTHY	Yes, in a sense. There's no need to be angry. It's just a word we use.
GEORGE	Yeah, yeah, I know about words.
DOROTHY	I know you do, Mr Leyburn.
GEORGE	I know about words, I'm a writer, Miss Headley.
DOROTHY	Of course you are.
GEORGE	I write 'em. I choose 'em, carefully, Miss Headley.
DOROTHY	Yes, I know.
GEORGE	Carefully.
DOROTHY	Mr Leyburn...
GEORGE	'Material'? 'Trim it for length?' This in't some bloody summer frock we're talking about!
DOROTHY	(VERY FIRMLY) Mr Leyburn, let me say this to you. You may choose to co-operate with me, or you may not, and that is of course your choice entirely. But if you refuse to allow me to revise your 'material' where necessary, for length or any other reason, then said 'material' will simply not be broadcast at all, and we shall both have wasted a great deal of each other's time, Mr Leyburn.
GEORGE	(GOING) Aye, well, I believe we shall have done. *PAUSE.*
DOROTHY	Good morning, Mr Leyburn.
GEORGE	(COMING BACK) Miss Headley, I...
DOROTHY	Yes?

GEORGE   I lost my temper and I...
DOROTHY   Yes?
GEORGE   I were rude to you, and...
DOROTHY   You're passionate about your work. So you should
            be.
GEORGE   I spoke out of turn. And I'm sorry.
DOROTHY   Your apology's accepted.

When George's story goes out on air, Dorothy's boss at the BBC, Alan Heathcote is less than keen.

HEATHCOTE   He's a gloomy little bugger, your George
                Leyburn.
DOROTHY   He isn't my George Leyburn, or, I expect,
                anybody else's.
HEATHCOTE   I must say, it's a cruel little story. I think it's
                rather nasty, rather sadistic. Is Leyburn
                married?
DOROTHY   Yes. I've met his wife.
HEATHCOTE   What's she like?
DOROTHY   One of the walking wounded.
HEATHCOTE   I shouldn't wonder at it. We've had a directive.
DOROTHY   Oh.
HEATHCOTE   Let me read it to you. 'We are, of course,
                recovering from a long and debilitating
                conflict. It is a time of moral and spiritual
                exhaustion. The nation needs at this time
                above all to be encouraged, strengthened, to
                have its collective heart raised. In short, and
                above all, may I say, it appears to me that the
                British people have a fervent desire, indeed a
                perfect right at this time in their history to be
                Cheered Up.'

The Alan Heathcotes of this world are still, sad to say, walking the corridors of the BBC to this day. Charles Parker owed his vision to producers and administrators who believed that programme-makers are the ones who know about making programmes. It is to be hoped that future Charles Parkers, and George Leyburns, will be given the chance of realising their vision through the extraordinarily flexible and powerful medium of radio.

Writing a Radio Sitcom
D.A. Barham

Why should I write a radio sitcom?

There are a number of reasons why people decide to write a radio sitcom. Becoming fabulously rich and famous is not, sadly, one of them. Insanity, redundancy and stupidity are three of the more popular reasons. Perhaps you're a drama writer wanting to try your hand at comedy – or a sketch-writer wanting to pen something more than 15 seconds in duration. Perhaps you're so appalled at the state of British sitcom that you reckon you could do much better. Or perhaps you're just on a 'creative roll', having recently dreamed up the expenses for your self-assessment tax form.

What's the difference between writing a sitcom for radio and writing a sitcom for TV?

About £100 a minute. Fortunately, for struggling writers at least, this means that a lot more sitcoms get made for radio than for TV. They also get made a lot more quickly. Little-known fact: when *Last of the Summer Wine* was first commissioned, it was about three twenty-somethings sharing a farmhouse, *Game On* style. Only by the time it actually aired the entire cast had reached pensionable age.

But for every radio sitcom that does reach transmission, there are a good half-dozen that don't. These are rejected after the recording of a 'pilot', or trial episode. Hence the dubbing of one hapless Light Entertainment trainee 'The Kamikaze Producer' (all his pilots went down without trace). It's this kind of sympathetic camaraderie that makes radio comedy so much fun to work in... Despite this wealth of opportunity, though, your chances of actually getting your sitcom made are slimmer than an anorexic stick insect's slim-fitting drainpipe trousers.

So why should I write for radio?

For that warm inner glow one always gets when doing good work for a near-hopeless charity cause? For the chance to obtain a coveted BBC ID card, allowing you to stroll into Broadcasting House, hang out with the likes of Libby Purves and purchase gritty BBC coffee?

Seriously, the benefits of radio as a medium for comedy cannot be overstressed (unlike radio comedy writers – who are frequently over stressed, largely due to money matters). Often referred to as the 'poor cousin' of television, it might be better likened to its drunken uncle. It gets away with more: it's frequently sick; it does some outrageous things after 11 pm (and it's particularly amusing over the Christmas holidays). Because, thanks to its lower budget, radio producers can afford to take risks – making one lousy series won't have wasted sufficient cash to feed an entire Third World nation on Beluga caviar for a year.

In stark contrast to TV, you won't be disappointed by the wobbly sets, the crappy special-effects or the lead actor looking like Len Fairclough when you'd imagined him as Leonardo di Caprio (as misty-eyed radio anoraks are so fond of saying 'aaah, the pictures are so much better on the wireless').

Most importantly, radio is a training ground for TV sitcom writers – think of it as a Sort of FA School of Excellence for the Wembley Stadium that is TV Centre. (Shouldn't be hard to visualize – there's no shortage of people talking balls.) Writing for radio is an excellent way to hone your sitcom skills before you naff off to America and make a million scripting the more successful follow-up to *Friends*. Which is, of course, what every radio writer secretly wants to do.

So what can you do on radio that you can't on TV?

My first sitcom was a prime example of something no TV producer would have touched with a ten-foot barge pole. Not because it wasn't funny (it wasn't particularly funny, but this has never stopped TV producers from commissioning a show), but because it was set, not in a cosy domestic setting with 2.4 children and a sofa, but in... a zoo. A whole menagerie of rare and dangerous livestock? On TV? A major undertaking, involving numerous animal-handlers, stringent safety precautions, hygiene officers, filming permission from Whipsnade, sincere assurances that no animals were harmed during the making of the programme and probably Rolf Harris on 24 hour standby just in case they were. To make the same show for radio? One 'Sounds Of The Jungle' FX disc and a couple of actors who can do the odd growling noise.

It's a similar situation with child actors. On radio, you can avoid the stress of working with a five-year-old stage-school brat with a string of Safeway ads under his belt, demanding to know his artistic motivation for saying the line 'Mu-uuuu-uuuuum..!' Instead, you can hire a 25-year-old penniless actor with a high-pitched voice and a low embarrassment threshold. Ditto with impressions. You want the Prime Minister, the Beatles, Prince Charles, Darth Vader and Shaggy from 'Scooby Doo' turning up on your main character's sofa? Fine! One half-decent impressionist shouldn't break the bank. Telly producers, however, would be wetting themselves to find suitable look-alikes, sound-alikes and cunning ways to blend live-action and animation techniques... and you'd probably end up having to rewrite the whole damn thing when they couldn't.

What are the limitations of radio?

Visual gags don't exactly go down a storm. Try closing your eyes and watching that video clip of David Jason's Del Boy leaning on the bar and toppling sideways (this is why radio writers have to be so much more skillful with their dialogue...). And magicians, mimes and ventriloquist acts aren't half so impressive. A friend of mine once made the mistake of submitting a space-based, futuristic sci-fi-com to Radio 4. Episode One featured – rib-ticklingly – an evil alien intruder which could metamorphose itself to both look and sound identical to any of the main characters... allowing for such comedically fertile scenarios as one character talking to his own doppelganger, whilst other characters failed to realise there was an extra-terrestrial impostor in their midst. And, of course, a very confused studio audience. This is a prime example of what not to do in a radio sitcom.

How do I get someone to read my script?

You don't. First mistake: you don't actually write your script yet. What you write at this stage is called a 'treatment' – a sort of advertisement, if you like, for your programme idea and your writing talents. The treatment usually consists of a brief synopsis of what the show is about (bonus points for including as many as possible of the following words: 'satirical', 'innovative', 'original' and 'Father Ted'), short potted biographies of the characters ('Patsy is a loud, chain-smoking alcoholic with a drug habit and no modesty') and a short potted biography of yourself ('Debbie is a loud, chain-smoking alcoholic with a drug habit and no modesty'). If possible, think up six scenarios, to show it's got series potential. This will probably take you a few hours – as opposed to the few months it could take to write the whole script, only to have it rejected on the basis that 'we've done hospital comedies, thanks. But if you have any other ideas which you feel may be suitable for the Department...'

If you *are* submitting a full, unsolicited script (and if you are, then you clearly have far too much time on your hands), then do remember to include a plain brown envelope. Stamped and self-addressed is preferable. Stuffed with used fivers can be surprisingly effective; but if you could afford that, then you wouldn't be a radio writer, would you?

Where do I start?

With an idea, with a character, with an interesting twist on a well-known scenario... With a desire to make people laugh... With a blank sheet of paper, a large overdraft and a copy of *The Writers' and Artists' Yearbook*, generally. You're unlikely to be writing a sitcom because someone is making it financially worth your while. You're writing a sitcom because of inspiration, motivation (and, frequently, intoxication) – the hard part is sustaining this motivation long enough to produce the whole script.

Do I need a funny title?

Building a whole show around a funny title is never the best way to start. Many of the most successful shows have the most unassuming titles – *Red Dwarf* was a sitcom set on a spaceship called, er... Red Dwarf. *Friends* was about... some friends, *Frasier* about a bloke called Frasier... Get my drift?

Producers won't reject or accept a sitcom on the title alone. One show I worked on was submitted to the network in treatment form with no title whatsoever. The proposal was simply headed 'The Treatment', and was rushed through so quickly that no-one remembered to think up a name for it. It's now been running for more than five years, entitled – yup, you've guessed it: *The Treatment*.

Where do my characters come from?

If you're Carla Lane? Liverpool. Otherwise... use your imagination. Base them on people you know, then exaggerate those people's most identifiable traits. (And change the names: radio money is far too measly to fund a libel case.) The most enduring comic personae are either flawed in some way, or permanently battling some kind of conflict (a vet who hates animals, a neurotic therapist, a sex-starved nymphomaniac, etc). Hence we have:

Basil (*Fawlty Towers*) Fawlty – working in the hospitality industry, but with the charm and social skills of Pol Pot.

Arnold (*Red Dwarf*) Rimmer – ruthlessly ambitious, but thwarted by the facts that he is (a) incompetent and (b) dead.

Corporal (*Dad's Army*) Jones – responsible for defending the realm, but liable to panic at a moment's notice.

Victor (*One Foot In The Grave*) Meldrew – miserable bastard.

Radio writers can be infinitely more creative here than TV writers – if your character has two heads, or the ability to fly, or a job that takes him to a different exotic location every week, you won't be obliged to rewrite for 'budget reasons', making him a one-headed accountant from Purfleet, Essex, whose job takes him to a different part of Purfleet, Essex, each week.

Do my characters have to be funny?

One flaw of many sitcom writers is believing that characters who spew forth a string of one-liners are automatically 'funny'. Not so! Unlike characters in 30-second sketches, characters in 30-minute sitcoms also need to be credible as people who can interact with each other and sustain the listener's interest for another five episodes. If all they do is spout gags, we never get to learn anything about their personality – and the listener will soon... Sorry! What were you saying? I think I must have dozed off.

Humour should come from the relationships between the main protagonists. (And no, by 'relationships' I don't just mean a lot of cheap knob gags or jokes about people losing their trousers. British comedy has moved on since the days of the 'Carry On' film.) It's important for the listener to sympathise with the main character – though this doesn't mean he or she has to be infallible. Victor Meldrew is a highly unlikeable man. But wouldn't you be, if you were in his shoes? And whilst Gordon Brittas is an unmitigated tosser, he's blissfully unaware of the fact. He thinks he's acting for the best of reasons, so we don't hate him – we just feel sorry for him. The same reason may explain why John Major managed to stay Prime Minister for quite as long as he did.

Help! I can do the 'com' bit, but all the good situations have been used!

... But not with your characters. Think about it – since when were drama writers deterred by the fact that 'someone else has already written something set in a hospital/police station/outer space'? Whilst radio does allow for more 'high concept' settings than TV, some of the most original sitcoms are set in the most mundane scenarios. Tying yourself down to a wacky premise ('the main character is a one-legged Feng Shui consultant married to a manic-depressive Belgian transvestite earning his living as a professional topless darts player. In a parallel universe. In the year 2056. When the rest of the human race has been wiped out and replaced by small green insects who communicate only by telepathy. Oh, and he's also a secret undercover spy') might sound funny for the first five minutes, but you'll soon be struggling to find fresh scenarios for your characters to be confronted with. Far better to say, 'It's about this bloke living in a flat' and explore the limitless range of funny situations he could find himself in from week to week.

Some bad sitcoms give the impression that the writer has simply stuck a pin in the good old Yellow Pages, thought, 'Aha! No-one's done a sitcom about sewerage clearance yet!' and scurried off to write 30 minutes of tedium entitled *Only Fouls And Hoses*. If you happen to have an interest in, enthusiasm for, or knowledge of sewerage clearance, then fine. You know the kind of humour sewage clearance workers use to relieve their boredom, their problems, their lifestyles, and the range of potentially amusing situations they might find themselves in. Your insight could make the subject interesting and funny. Otherwise, write about something a little closer to your heart (word of warning, though – struggling writers are another topic that's been done to death...)

However 'original' your situation, some other git will invariably have had the same idea. The latest edition of the BBC Writers' Guidelines lists the following situations as currently over-exploited: road protesters, football clubs, the Internet, history, ancient Rome, space, dream worlds, the afterlife and middle-aged women who suddenly find themselves single again and struggle to find independence. So steer clear of those, and you're that bit further from the producer's slush-pile. At the end of the day though, it's the characters, not the situation, that will swing whether your script gets the go-head.

Characters... Situation... What next?

Your next step is to break down the plot of the first episode into ten or so separate scenes. Briefly outline what will happen in each. Imagine you're writing a 'crib guide' to your sitcom for particularly dim GCSE students. Then make it even simpler, so that the average Light Entertainment producer can understand it. The breakdown will help you iron out any inconsistencies early on, rather than have the lead actor tap you politely on the shoulder five minutes before the recording starts, asking, 'But hang on – didn't my character get fatally shot on page five?' It will also avoid your writing the whole script, only to have it returned by the producer saying it's 'absolutely hilarious' but he doesn't like the plot, so could you start again please. The breakdown for the first scene of *The Elephant Man*, Episode I, went something along the lines of 'Scene I. We meet the main characters (Terry and Leonard) at the zoo where they work. Establish that the zoo is in deep financial doo-doo. Introduce the domineering boss, Stephanie, and set up the main plot – that there is a new, rare animal arriving soon to boost visitor numbers.' As you can see, the synopsis doesn't have to include any jokes (though if you think of any which might be relevant to any particular scene, write them down now before you forget them). It's purely for your benefit, and to convince the producer that you do have some, vaguely coherent idea about what he's paying you to write.

Tell me more about plotting.

Plotting is a key part of sitcom writing. Plotting to kill the producer, actors and/or studio audience, in most cases. The other type of plotting is far more complex and unrewarding, and involves constructing a coherent storyline for your characters. A plot can basically be divided into three main strands.

Introduction – we establish that there is a problem, or conflict.
Development – the problem is exacerbated.
Conclusion – but somehow it is finally resolved.

Each episode will hopefully have one main plot, and one or two subsidiary plots running alongside it. Frequently, the main storyline is completely encapsulated in one episode, whilst other themes continue throughout the series. For example – one episode of *The Elephant Man* evolved around Terry's birthday. The birthday plot was played out completely within the one episode, whilst simultaneously, the 'struggling zoo lurching ever-closer to financial ruin' plot took another step towards conclusion. There was also, in this episode, a running joke about Terry's receding hairline. 'Runners', as they're known, are another good way to make the listener feel they really know a particular character. Even if they've not listened to any of the previous episodes.

Don't forget the plot in your enthusiasm to cram in as many gags as possible. A sitcom with no plot is just as bad as a sitcom with no jokes, but you can't fob the former off as 'alternative comedy' – it's just lazy writing. When John Cleese and Connie Booth wrote *Fawlty Towers*, they spent far longer honing the plot than they did writing gags. The results speak for themselves – if you've got an inventive, watertight plot and convincing characters, the jokes should start to evolve all by themselves. Don't expect it to be easy. Evolution is a long, slow process.

I'm itching to get into the dialogue...

Once you and your producer have agreed on a one-page synopsis of events in each episode, then you can finally go away and write it. Trust me, it'll be all the better for the pre-planning.

How do I actually write the dialogue, then?

So you've got your finger quivering eagerly over the keyboard and a large supply of the finest powdered Columbian-grown stimulants on tap (writers are single-handedly responsible for sustaining 90% of the world's coffee-producers). But the first line of a sitcom is like the first sentence of a novel. It's more painful to extract than a Rottweiler's wisdom teeth. My tip? Since you know roughly what's going to happen as your plot progresses, why not start with an 'easier' scene? Let the characters come alive in your head. Then, when they're swapping witty repartee like old friends, go back and grapple with the dreaded Scene One. With a bit of luck, you'll know your protagonists so well now that they'll practically write it themselves. And hey, they won't even expect a cut of the money. Now that's what I call a deal.

Everyone writes in a different way. When I wrote that first scene of the first episode of my first sitcom, I guess I copped out. I didn't begin with a line at all. I began with a sound effect. It wasn't even a funny sound effect. It was:

    I. F/X   CAR DOOR SLAMS.

Since I can tell you're dying to know what happened next, here's how that first scene of Episode One expanded to fill the first few minutes of air time.

    SCENE I. ZOO. DAY ONE.

    1. F/X   CAR DOOR SLAMS.
    2. LEONARD   EMOTIONAL Erm... listen... I know I'm not

very good at expressing my feelings but... this could be the last time we ever see each other. I just wanted to tell you... well, we've had some good times together. I wish it didn't have to end this way.

3. F/X   CAMEL SNORTS. TRAILER DOOR SLAMS SHUT.

4. LEONARD   You will remember to give her plenty of fresh fruit?

5. DRIVER   Don't you worry, Mr McCann. We've three other camels at Chester. She'll be well looked after.

6. LEONARD   And you won't forget to talk to her? I allus talk to my animals. Been sharing my problems with that there camel for... och, nigh on twelve years now.

7. DRIVER   Yeah? Thought she looked a bit down in the mouth. I put it down to intestine trouble.

8. F/X ENGINE STARTS UP, REVS OFF.

9. TERRY   APPROACHING Well, I suppose that's one less heap of dung to shovel up tomorrow morning...

10. LEONARD   COLDLY Oh, there you are, Terry. I thought you'd decided to knock off early.

11. TERRY   Honestly, Leonard, we can't go on like this. We've sold off half the zoo and our bank balance is still redder than a baboon's backside. Leonard?

12. LEONARD   Aye?

13. TERRY   Have you been listening to anything I've just said?

14. LEONARD   Aye.

15. TERRY   It's just that you seem a bit... well, more miserable than usual. And your eyes look all red. You haven't been –

16. LEONARD   SNIFFS. CURTLY. I've just got a bit of a cold, that's all.

17. TERRY   Ah. Sorry. I knew drugs weren't really your scene.

18. F/X   HEELS CLICKING ON CONCRETE APPROACHING.

19. TERRY   Uh-oh. Here she comes. Stalin in stilettos...

20. STEPHANIE   CLAPS HANDS Chop-chop! No slacking, you two! If this place isn't looking shipshape,

	no-one will come to see it, will they?
21. LEONARD	They don't anyway, Miss Stonewick. More people have seen the Loch Ness Monster. Kids these days want Sonic Hedgehogs and Ninja Turtles. All we've got is a catatonic warthog and some miserable monkeys.
22. STEPHANIE	Aha! Speaking of monkeys... Terence. Can you load that young male chimpanzee into the trailer before you lock up? He's leaving tomorrow.
23. TERRY	Is there something wrong with him?
24. STEPHANIE	He attacked the jaguar again last week.
25. LEONARD	What! I was never told! Is the jaguar alright?
26. STEPHANIE	Just a scratch. But he could have had the aerial clean off, never mind the heated wing-mirrors.
27. TERRY	Miss Stonewick, there's no way this can go on. The animals can sense that there's something wrong. That laughing hyena's starting to look like Nigel Mansell. If business doesn't pick up soon we'll have to close down.
27. STEPHANIE	Not necessarily, Terence. I think I just might have come up with a solution. BEAT Look at London Zoo. Made a fortune last year from that Chinese panda. What we need at Southwood is our own... Gang-Bang.
28. TERRY	Ming-Ming.
29. STEPHANIE	Whatever. Then we go the whole hog on publicity.
30. LEONARD	ASIDE We sold the whole hog to Whipsnade, remember?
31. STEPHANIE	Listen, you miserable specimen, what I'm trying to get through to your bug-sized brain is the way London Zoo marketed that panda... they had panda posters, panda pencils, even panda pants! And they sold! I mean, panda pants! What kind of sad, pathetic individual would wear –
32. TERRY	HURRIEDLY Er, look – there's no way we've got the resources to keep a giant panda here.
33. STEPHANIE	It doesn't have to be a panda, Terence! We just need something... unusual.
34. TERRY	I've got a genuine lock of Desmond Morris's hair.
35. STEPHANIE	In fact, it's arriving tomorrow. The Peruvian

> hairy leafhopper. One of the world's rarest
> animals...

... And so it continued. OK, it's not exactly Chekov. But in a matter of minutes, we've accomplished the following essential tasks which will – hopefully – keep the listener hooked for eight episodes. We have:

a. Introduced the main characters, and their defining characteristics. It's already clear that Leonard is dour, Scottish and pessimistic, but with a caring side – at least where animals are concerned. Terry, meanwhile, is more laid-back and cheerful, and Stephanie Stonewick is a despotic, hard-nosed boss who makes Margaret Thatcher look like Ma Walton. Thus we can already sympathise with Terry, having such a motley assortment of colleagues – and we've not even met them all yet.

b. Established that the zoo has problems. This is the long-running plot which will develop over the course of the whole series.

c. Introduced a potential solution to the problem – the arrival of a new 'star exhibit'. This is the main plot of Episode One, which will be developed and resolved in the next thirty minutes. (You want to know what happens? Write to the BBC, demanding an immediate repeat of all eight programmes.)

d. We might have made the audience giggle a couple of times, even if it was just with the rather unlikely camel noise in cue 3.

How do I make it funny?

That's the tricky bit. For a start, everyone has their own idea of what 'funny' is. A vicar losing his trousers in a Ray Cooney farce? Small children swearing gratuitously in South Park? Your best bet is to write what makes you laugh, and hope others share your sense of humour – however warped it may be.

Don't listen to all those earnest types who try to 'analyse' comedy – airily proclaiming such theories as, 'There are only seven actual jokes in existence'. Analysing comedy is a sure-fire way to render it devoid of any amusement value. Why is the number '57' funnier than the number '14'? Why is 'Oswestry' funnier than 'Darlington'?

The pros have developed a few nifty ways of doing 'funny' without resorting to crow-barring in a couple of hoary old gags every time the laugh level needs a bit of oomph. Take *Blackadder*, for instance. Ben Elton inserted ludicrous comparatives every couple of pages – which might be easier than Ebeneezer Easy's Easy-Listening Album, but it stopped the dialogue from becoming as turgid as that of many other sitcoms. Victoria Wood realised the comic potential of household brand names – a 'Fray Bentos Individual Chicken and Ham Shortcrust' being so much funnier than a mere 'pie'. And catchphrases are always, to coin a phrase – a cunning plan. The secret is knowing how not to over-egg the pudding; none of the above is a substitute for genuinely witty dialogue.

The best tip I can give is to always keep a notebook handy (I prefer the paper sort, but if you're more technically inclined, a Compaq or Toshiba would do the job just as well). When a joke suddenly hits you out of the blue – or you find yourself standing in the supermarket queue behind someone who'd be the perfect foil for your lead character – you can jot the idea down before it passes you by. You don't even need the notebook – simply carrying a pen will do. Scribble half-formed gags down on the loo roll, on a restaurant napkin, on your own arm...

Sound effects are always funny, aren't they?

FX: SLAPS HEAD

Doh! Another common failing. Relying too heavily on sound effect gags is a bad move on two scores: firstly, it gives the impression that you can't actually write a funny line; and secondly, it assumes that the sound effects 'department' (generally one harassed studio manager with a tray of gravel, some coconut shells, and a CD entitled *The Best BBC Sound Effects CD In The World... Ever!*) can produce something sufficiently risible to convey your joke to a weary audience. Setting my sitcom in a zoo was asking for trouble: I don't think there's a big demand for FX: *GIANT PANDAS COPULATING* or FX: *HIPPO SITS ON SKODA CAR* in the normal, day-to-day run of things. And there certainly isn't much call for colic-stricken rhinoceroses in *The Archers*. (Merely obtaining the sound of a perfectly ordinary, non-hippo-related car reversing, stopping and having the door opened took three retakes.)

That isn't to say that a well-placed sound effect can't have the requisite 'hilarious consequences'. And sound effects can add a lot to a sitcom, even if they're not 'funny' in themselves. Think back to Douglas Adams' seminal *Hitch Hiker's Guide To The Galaxy*, way back in the mists of ancient time (well, 1977, to be precise). Producer Geoffrey Perkins used the marvels of the BBC Radiophonic Workshop to try to recreate what was going on in Douglas's fevered imagination. The FX weren't, necessarily, mind-bogglingly amusing as such; but the fantastical soundscape they built up made the show sound like no comedy before or since. The result was a radio classic – and further proof of the medium's superiority over TV. The television version, whilst just as funny in term of scripts, was ruined by the cheap-looking sets, ridiculous 'aliens' and dubious prosthetic heads.

How long should it take me to write each episode?

How long is a piece of string (or 'shoestring', in the case of the average radio sitcom budget)? If you're unlucky, your sitcom will already have been placed in the schedules, so if you haven't written it by then... well, you'd better start brushing up your improvisational skills and/or employ a very large bodyguard.

All writers work at different speeds. Jeffrey Archer can churn out a work of humorous fiction in mere days (less, if it's a really urgent legal testimonial), whilst others toil for years over just the one book (Norris McWhirter being a prime example). Sitcom writers are the same. I've known those who can write a whole episode in a weekend; and I've know one who spent six years writing five episodes (it started off as a futuristic space-com a la *Red Dwarf* and ended up as historical hysteria in the *Blackadder* mould).

Write at a pace which you're happy with. A scene a day keeps the producer away... Ten pages a day... Or spend the whole day fiddling with the margins and finding a pretty logo to go on the cover page. It's up to you. And your bank manager.

Anything I really shouldn't do?

A common affliction of radio writers (third only to malnutrition and alcohol dependency) is to be too 'wordy': deprived of the opportunity to use visual humour, they feel compelled to explain every gag in minute detail, just to ensure that even the stupidest, most comedically-challenged person in the room (again, this is generally the producer) can 'get it'. Jokes work best when they're short and snappy – and they're also easy for the actors to deliver without the benefit of the long rehearsal times enjoyed by their TV colleagues. Again, it's impossible to offer a hard and fast rule on the subject, but if you find your jokes are taking three pages per gag, then either you're being too wordy or your font is way too big.

Unlike sketch-writers, sitcom writers have to make the listener believe in their characters. Even if you *have* got a rip-snortingly funny, X-rated line about three nuns with a baguette on a bike on a cobbled street, putting such a gag in the mouth of a priest would hardly be realistic. Or maybe it would... That all depends on the type of priest you've created. It doesn't matter how outrageous their personalities, as long as your characters are consistent.

Instead of 30 seconds, you've got 30 minutes to engage the listener's attention. And whereas a sketch writer will have to set his scene up within the first couple of sentences, you have no excuse for exchanges such as the following:

FX:	KNOCK AT DOOR. DOOR OPENED.
MR BROWN:	Aaaargh! My darling wife Mrs Brown! How unexpected of you to return home from your evening class in eighteenth century basket-weaving techniques at precisely the moment I happen to be hanging from the chandelier with our semi-naked cleaning lady, devoid of under garments and with a crevice-tool Hoover attachment inserted up my rectal passage.
MRS BROWN:	Doh!

FADE OUT ON HUGE LAUGH FROM LOBOTOMISED TV STUDIO AUDIENCE.

The successful radio sitcom writer will have built up this scenario over several pages of cleverly-plotted dialogue and acutely-observed characterisation. When the denouement finally comes, all it will need is:

FX:	KNOCK AT DOOR. DOOR OPENED. PAUSE.

MRS BROWN: Doh!

FADE OUT ON HUGE LAUGH FROM SLIGHTLY MORE
SOPHISTICATED RADIO STUDIO AUDIENCE.

If you've created a convincing enough picture in the listener's mind,
the hilarity of the situation should be as clear as anything any TV set-
designer could dream up.

Doctor, doctor! I think I'm suffering from writer's block!

Don't sit staring at a blank screen, waiting for inspiration to come. It
won't. Turn off your PC and go and do something less boring instead.
Douglas Adams used to swear by taking a bath every time he was short
of ideas; though taking a bath is, obviously, a pretty radical concept for
your average scummy pen-pusher. And if you are going to employ this
novel tactic, remember: unplug the computer before you get in.

Yippee! I've finished my script. What do I do now?

Stuff it in the back of your sock drawer and go down the boozer. No,
honestly. The last thing you should do right now is give it to your
producer. Leave it for at least a couple of days. Then (when you need
a clean pair of socks) re-read it. Trust me, you'll be astounded at just
how unfunny it is. Go through and rewrite all the worst bits. Then
hand it over to your producer!

Is that it, then? Time to sit back and relax?

Nope. Time to sit back and *rewrite*.
     Your producer will inevitably have reservations about the script. It
will, inevitably, be returned to you covered in red marks. You will,
inevitably, be aghast. How dare this snivelling, worm-like individual
criticise your gems of comedic brilliance? And you'll be sorely tempted
to inform him just where he can stick his 'needs a better punch-line',
his 'too convoluted' and his 'is this supposed to be a joke? Please
explain'.
     Restrain yourself. Humour this miserable specimen. Smile benignly
and trot off to dutifully remove all the funniest bits of your script, as

per his specifications. The reason for doing re-writes is again, very simple – money. You don't get paid the second half of your fee until your script has been 'accepted'. I've only ever witnessed one sure-fire way of avoiding re-writes, and this was by a writer who was so late delivering his script that he was actually writing it during the recording. However, this is not advisable. Actors' nerves are on a par with those of thoroughbred racehorses.

Can we go and record it now?

When you ask your producer for 'feedback' on the script, this is precisely what he (or she) will produce. Producer-speak is a language completely unlike modern English. It will take the aspiring sitcom-writer a while to master such a complex tongue, so here are a few handy words and phrases to get you started.

YOUR PRODUCER:	Well, I've read your script through several times,,,
TRANSLATION.	Well, I've been using your script as a door jamb for several months now. This morning I saw your name in my diary and hastily skim-read it in the lift.
YOUR PRODUCER:	In general I'm very happy with it.
TRANSLATION:	... As a door jamb.
YOUR PRODUCER:	However, there are a few little niggles that occurred to me.
TRANSLATION:	I hated it.
YOUR PRODUCER:	Now I'm no writer, but...
TRANSLATION:	... But I've always wanted to be. So I'm going to hack your carefully-structured gags about like nobody's business.
YOUR PRODUCER:	It's more of a comedy drama, wouldn't you say?
TRANSLATION:	It's not funny.
YOUR PRODUCER:	Could you maybe reword the punchline to the artichoke joke on page 17?
TRANSLATION:	It's not funny.
YOUR PRODUCER:	Some of the gags are quite... slow-burning...

TRANSLATION:	It's not funny.
YOUR PRODUCER:	You're intending this to be a non-audience show, yes?
TRANSLATION:	It's not funny.
YOUR PRODUCER:	I absolutely loved the... title.
TRANSLATION:	It's not funny.

Like Eskimos and rain, producers have at least 57 different words for saying 'not funny'. If your producer laughs heartily at the first draft, proclaiming it the new Hancock – be afraid. Be very, very afraid. This means it's not funny, and you might as well go back and start from scratch.

Where can I get canned laughter from?

Contrary to popular belief, the laughter in radio sitcoms actually comes from real people.

The benefits of having an audience:

•   The buzz you get from making 300 people crease up with helpless laughter. Without having to resort to removal of your undergarments.
•   Reassurance that it *is*, in fact, funny.
•   The knowledge that you're providing 300 assorted ne'er-do-wells with shelter from the elements for at least thirty minutes. You can then feel less guilty about the next 300 homeless people who you don't buy *The Big Issue* from.
•   People won't listen to your show under the assumption that it is a serious drama, or piece of gritty social reportage. I swear, there must have been those who tuned in to *The Elephant Man* expecting a harrowing tale of a bloke with a hideously disfiguring facial growth. (Then again, Radio 2 was always popular with Barry Manilow fans.)
•   Your producer is less likely to edit out your favourite line, if it got a big guffaw on the tape.
•   You've got someone to hide behind when it all starts to go horribly wrong.

The drawbacks of having an audience:

• They might laugh in the wrong place. They might not laugh at all, in which case you will have to call it a 'comedy drama' and make sure the word 'whimsical' appears somewhere in the *Radio Times* billing. 'Whimsical' is, of course, another synonym for 'not funny'.

• They might all be aspiring sitcom-writers, out to steal your jokes.

• Radio budgets rarely stretch to providing a warm-up man, so pre-show entertainment is generally limited to a few weak jokes from your producer (revelling in his big chance to do stand-up comedy in front of a live audience). After attending all six episodes, even the most sympathetic comedy-groupie will probably have tired of the line '... And a word about fire arrangements. We've arranged the fire for half-past seven...' Copious retakes and breaks in recording, therefore, are a luxury you can't really afford. The audience will merely get bored, walk out, make loud, rude remarks or start rustling packets of smelly fish-paste sandwiches and putting the actors off their cues.

• A small audience sounds far worse than no audience at all. Twelve people tittering nervously in a 300-seater theatre can only ever sound like twelve people, no matter how hard you lean on the volume knob. Everyone assumes it's 'canned laughter' anyway.

What are the worst mistakes a sitcom writer can make?

• Stealing someone else's jokes. Amongst comedy professionals, theft of jokes is about the worst sin imaginable. Kids – don't do it. (It's perfectly possible for two writers to have thought of the same odd line independently – but lifting entire chunks of John Cleese's dialogue and replacing the names 'Basil Fawlty' and 'Manuel' with 'Bernard Farquar-Up' and 'Pablo' is a bit of a give-away.)

• Including stage-directions such as *PAN ACROSS THE ROOM TO REVEAL BROWN'S CAST-OFF UNDERWEAR HANGING OVER THE PARROT CAGE* or *BLACKOUT*. These are a dead give-away that your script was rejected by the TV producers and you can't even be faffed to re-write it for a radio audience.

• Writing what is, essentially, a stand-up act split between half a dozen different speakers. The one exception to the rule was Larry Seinfeld: setting his character up as a professional stand-up comedian gave him a reason to wisecrack at every opportunity.

• Assuming that swear words are automatically funny. They are not.

You will realise this when the producer uses them in reference to you and/or your script, whilst throwing it in the bin and stamping on it.
• I was told to write three gags per page. Is this correct? Of course there's no rule governing jokes-per-minute. Whilst there are still those who abide by the old 'three gags per page' maxim, you can happily ignore them. They are mad. They are the same people who abide by other old maxims, such as, 'The best things come to those who wait'. Which – as your producer will inform you, when you fail to deliver your script on time – is also a pile of pants.

The three-gags-per-page rule is not just unworkable, it was also dreamed up before the advent of Microsoft Word. Any producer foolish enough to apply it these days is more than likely to find himself presented with a script five pages long, printed in 0.8-point Courier font with half-a-millimetre line spacing and no margins.

So how many gags *should* you allow per page? One? Ten? Fifteen knob jokes, twelve satirical jibes, five puns, three clever-though-not-particularly-amusing literary allusions and one hoary old chestnut shamelessly nicked? Write what you think is the funniest script you can produce.
• No matter how hilarious your dialogue, there will always be some humourless half-wit who doesn't get the joke and reckons he could write a far funnier script himself. This person is known in radio terms as 'the Producer'. And in writers' terms as something far too unchivalrous to be mentioned in a publication such as this.

I want to do it with my best friend.

Good idea? Co-writing is a popular practice amongst sitcom-writers – with plenty of successful partnerships in evidence (Croft and Perry, Marks and Gran, Clement and La Frenais). The big advantage is that if it's not funny, you can blame your co-writer's lack of talent; whilst if it's a huge success, you can claim all the credit. The down-side is that your co-writer will do precisely the same thing.

Think very carefully before writing with someone you know well. The intense, often turbulent relationship between co-writers could spoil a beautiful friendship: at least one successful comedy-writing duo are now only speaking through their lawyers.
Any final tips?

Always bear in mind the golden rule of radio sitcom writing: 'He who laughs last... doesn't get the joke'. You are funny, whatever anyone else might think. Hold that thought. Radio sitcom-writing might not make you a big household name (unless you write under the pseudonym Mister Sheen or Dom S. Doss), but watching 300 people enjoy a simultaneous knee-trembler of a gag – and knowing it was your gag – is one hell of a thrill. And hey, it beats having a real job. Convinced? OK, now go away and write, goddammit!

A LIFE THROUGH RADIO
Sam Boardman-Jacobs

This is the story of how a child from a council estate in Birmingham, through the medium of radio, fell foul of the Secret Police in post-Ceausescu Romania. I remember darkness and I remember sounds from the highly polished, family radio set, now a treasured item on a shelf above my writing desk. Throughout my childhood it was my educator and my companion. From its hessian covered speaker, to the glow of it's green eye, I was 'exposed' to the plays of William Shakespeare and of Max Frisch.

Once, when left alone to listen to *Journey Into Space*, I hid behind the settee and shuddered with fear as the characters reacted with vocal terror to their first sighting of the space monster. That mind-picture of a monster that I created for myself has never been surpassed by any special effect in a horror film. *Larry the Lamb*'s adventures in Toytown were cosier and I had no problems accepting that a woollen lamb talked, albeit with a rather pronounced 'bleat' – and a posh bleat at that – to a toy policeman. Then there were the rather refined early 1950s West End Theatre hits about the doings of the middle classes. I had never met a middle class person so I had to take their voices on trust, the space monster was easier to picture. In one of those London successes I heard the word 'cutlet'. What the hell was a cutlet? My parents had no idea. The word became synonymous with elegance and culture. *Look Back in Anger* had yet to arrive in the British theatre and shake the French windows out of their frames.

But before the theatre gave us real working-class characters, radio-drama was doing just that. I recall a stunning play from that era about a fire in a London clothing-manufacturer's sweatshop. The leading actors – whom I later discovered, were stars of The London Yiddish Theatre, Lilly Kahn and Meir Tzinkler – portrayed working class

Jewish characters recognisably like my own relatives. That play also managed to imbue me with the history and principles of the early trade union movement. There was fire again in the Max Frisch play *The Fire Raisers*, a memorable performance from that greatly underrated actor Alfred Marks. Alfred was later to star in several of my own radio plays. In fact, he played characters based on my own father so often that, when Alfred died, I felt bereaved all over again. His portrayal of my father was more real than the sadly lacking performance of my own dad.

But back then, as a child of the Second World War living in two freezing-cold inner city rooms, existing on a meagre austerity-diet of greyish-tinged dehydrated mashed potatoes and nary a 'cutlet' in sight, I could not conceive of mixing and mingling with these God-like personages. In our rationed, grey post-war lives, for body-warmth we had the fireplace and for mind-warmth we had the 'Wireless'. Thirty-odd years later, when I walked into the faded Art Deco grandeur of BBC Radio's Broadcasting House, it was as if I were walking into my childhood longings. Definitely a 'cutlet' zone.

Although I was arriving as a new radio-drama playwright, it was hard not to become that Birmingham slum child again. I fully expected the uniformed commissionaire to grab my collar and turf me out into Langham Place. Instead, I was led through the corridors that Tommy Handley, Arthur Askey and 'Stinker' Murdoch had walked, past the ghosts of Ben Lyon and Bebe Daniels Lyon and Dick Barton, the fire-damaged Grace Archer and the truly troubled Mrs Dale. I am sure that today's child would experience the same wonder on visiting the Television Centre, the crucial difference being that the modern TV-reared child will know what their stars look like. Mine lived inside my head.

I began with a comedy about gay criminals called *Slow Twisting*. That was the unsolicited script that caused me to be summoned to Broadcasting House for the first time. I sat, trying to cover my frayed shirt-cuffs with my too-short jacket sleeves, as the producer praised my script to the skies:

'Everybody in the drama department has read it. We all laughed until we cried. You're the funniest writer we've read in a long time. Original, witty, subversive...' I smirked, trying to look modest yet subversive.

The producer continued:

'However we won't be broadcasting it.'

'Sorry?'

'It's too subversive, and rather immoral. We couldn't possibly broadcast a play about a group of gay crooks.' I gulped.

'But if you come up with anything else we would be very interested.'

I leave the building.

A month later I am back with a play about two nutty old people who build a glider in their attic and crash land it on the Cenotaph during the Remembrance Day service. I had clearly read too many books that declared that 'anything was possible in radio-drama'. Well it wasn't, not then, and they didn't want it. Two months later I arrived to get the verdict on the first draft of a play based on a true story about two women prisoners in Ravensbruck concentration camp which also included the character of Franz Kafka, some implicit Lesbianism and a brief but unpleasant bout of necrophilia. (I wish to this day that someone had made me cut it, but we learn these lessons the hard way.)

Secure by now in the cosiness of rejection, I again sat in the same office with the same producer and sipped the obligatory plastic cup of BBC coffee. 'How long did this take you?'

I decided to lie: 'Two months.'

In fact I had written it in a non-stop ten-day, chain-smoking burst during which even the cat tried to leave home. The BBC bought *Her Name Was Milena* and broadcast it. It later went to Israeli Radio where, I am reliably told, it has been broadcast so often on Holocaust Memorial Day that many young Israelis remember being forced to listen to it and now loathe it with a passion.

The powers-that-be decided I was a 'fresh new talent' with a 'European vision'. I know for a fact that the only place from which I could have got a European vision, was a lifetime of listening to radio-drama.

I spent the next few years having two to three 90-minute radio plays a year broadcast. Then I was told by my producer that I 'wrote too much'.

I think he meant that I was wearing him out. I had been set upon a course of expanding the medium. The play I wrote about the Spanish Civil War and bullfighting was so complex in sound terms and had required so much post-production editing and multi-tracking that the sound engineer involved in the technical work reputedly paid off his mortgage with the overtime he earned. Even then the tapes were only just ready on the day of the first broadcast. Today it would be the producer alone with his SADIE computer editing programme. Then I had even travelled to Madrid and sat in the bullring with a tape recorder on my lap to capture the authentic sound of a corrida. It sounded as if it had been recorded through the lavatory window and was replaced with a stock sound-effect disk.

I followed this with an epic play about the Israeli-Palestinian conflict. The producer and I travelled to Israel to capture the sounds for this piece. (Should anyone from BBC finance be reading this, we also made a rather successful documentary feature when we were there, honest!) I think it was whilst, at my insistence, he was hanging over the dock wall at Jaffa, me holding on to his feet, while he dangled a microphone above the surf to capture the authentic sound of the incoming Mediterranean sea, that he decided he had had enough. Or could it have been the ten takes in the hired Israeli taxi that involved slamming on the brakes inches before a hairpin bend that finally cracked his nerve?

A few weeks later, that producer was at a Sony radio award lunch and happened to be sitting next to the then producer of *The Archers*. She happened to mention she was looking for new writers. The next day I was having a drink with her in a London Hotel bar, telling her how I had been listening to the programme since the first broadcast. (I suspect I may even have given her the impression that I was a humble farmer's son from Warwickshire.) Whatever I said, it must have had the right effect, for two days later I was attending my first script meeting at BBC Pebble Mill where I stayed to write over 600 episodes. Radio-drama travels better than you might think. I can recall crouching under a reinforced desk in a Jerusalem rabbi's wife's study, at the end of the Six Day War listening to an episode of *The Archers* on short wave. British radio-drama writing expertise is now highly exportable. In both the former Soviet satellites and third world, radio writing is in demand. This isn't just because radio is cheaper than television. If you have a large and poor population, a fledgling democracy and, in Romania's case, a new economic and political way of living and a population who have never experienced functioning democracy and economic choices, then radio-drama can be the answer.

I went to Bucharest as part of a joint initiative between the BBC World Service and the European Union. The team's brief was to train the local production crew to produce, write and direct their first ever home grown soap. The soap's job was to demonstrate, through good drama, the consequences of participating or not in a voters' society. My job was to train the writers. Modern European dramatists are used to writing with no censorship. It was a shock therefore to discover that contemporary Romanian dramatists used a style of allegory and metaphor that was opaque even to a Romanian audience. They called this style 'wooden words'. Years of terror and oppression, with secret police informers everywhere, had resulted in a style of talking and writing which was totally noncommittal: nothing was ever allowed to seem to mean anything! Fine for surviving Ceausescu's whims; useless for conveying soap stories. The radio station of Radio Romania was of the same vintage as my family's radio set. It hadn't, however, benefited from my mother's regular polishings. Almost nothing had been modernised. There were no computers, no light bulbs, no toilet paper. I found a single paper clip, in a crack of the office floorboards. Guiltily I took it. I had just stolen the only paper clip in Radio Romania! Rumour had it that in the basement was a computer. This had been cobbled together from rejected Bulgarian spare parts. Nobody however had actually seen it and we certainly weren't given access.

The Radio Romania studios were a living history of radio-drama, barely preserved in dust. Radio-drama teachers feature strongly the invention of the 'dramatic mixing panel', a means of mixing (then live) sound from several studios at once, giving radio-drama the fluidity of cinema. Here it was preserved in the studios, patterned in veneered wood, a producer's control room that overlooked several studios at once. The recording equipment was vintage East German. The tape store room, full of ancient tapes in rotting cardboard boxes supervised by a large woman clad in pink, knitting incessantly with pink wool. In the top floor canteen, there was no food. Exhausted by the climb – I didn't trust that lift – I sat down. The canteen chair crumbled to dust beneath me. In this ancient dusty ruin we had to create a modern vibrant radio soap opera.

I had no illusions that we were wanted there. In exchange for enduring our foreign intrusion, they would receive and have installed a state of the art modern studio set up. The script conference was fed by black market food from the interpreter's rucksack; bread, cheese, salami. The paper filters for the coffee machine caused greater problems. The Romanian producer vanished for four hours to return triumphant waving German coffee filter papers, purchased at a suburban hairdressing salon. Ice cube trays were available in one style, large shocking pink rubber moulds in the shape of female breasts imported from Bulgaria.

Ionesco is Romanian after all!

I worked on the producer's lap-top. Unfortunately, the printer was still held up in customs, so we passed the lap top, with the storylines, round the table of writers. The writers were more interested in the glittering technological bauble than the storylines. The average salary for a professional person in Romania was the equivalent of one hundred dollars. The cost of living was rapidly rising to meet European levels. Most of the writers had several jobs. The most famous of them, a celebrated local playwright, was eagerly awaiting his visa to Canada where he intended to become a dustman. In this atmosphere we had to tackle the pressing issues of the society.

We had to convey the problems caused by prejudice against Gypsies, Jews and Gays. We had to demonstrate the positive aspects of using one's democratic vote, the disadvantages of throwing your rubbish from the sixth floor of a block of flats (a serious problem in urban Bucharest where several people had been maimed: a woman had her shoulder broken by a falling orange). We also had to dramatise abandoned children – the product of Ceausescu's total ban on abortion. In Romania, abortion was the normal method of contraception. Another pressing issue was the packs of rabid wild dogs that roamed the centre of the city. The producer had been attacked by these dogs and had beaten them off with a large bag full of old *Archers* scripts. A country that had been gutted and exploited by a dictatorship was now in danger of being exploited by foreign investment. This was a long way from Ambridge and Brookside Close.

We not only had to create these storylines, we had to introduce humour and warmth, tell it all from a human angle and locate it in a recognisable neighbourhood of contemporary inner city Bucharest. The Romanian writers had no doubts about the problem. They announced en masse at the first script meeting that,

'It won't work! It's totally impossible!'

I could see how, from their perspective, it would seem impossible. They had not, like me, grown up on a diet of BBC radio-drama. They had not experienced the change of consciousness of the urban population to the problems of British farmers struggling with post-war problems. *The Archers,* as was its brief, had achieved that and more. It was partly because of the success of this social experiment in drama that we were there at all.

I drew upon my childhood and adolescent listening, as well as my experiences writing for *The Archers* and *Brookside.* Forty years of radio-drama listening had its effect. I searched back for the universal that reached me in my Birmingham council flat. The soap had to be believable to people in different regions of the country; we could not portray a capital city impression of the provinces. The script meetings were almost violent. The local writers revealed their contempt for contemporary soaps. We then discovered that their experience of soaps were imported Latin and North American TV soaps on satellite TV. Pure consumer escapism. Although, as we pointed out to the team, they had played their part in bringing down the Iron Curtain by beaming impossible images of capitalist consumption to populations starved of consumer goods. When we showed them our 'educational' style of social realist drama, they were even more horrified. 'Soviet propaganda!' was their response. We soon learned to avoid any scene which started with a factory sound effect. It was too reminiscent of Russian style 'Boy meets tractor' propaganda drama. We had been so concerned to assure them we were not there to make propaganda for Western capitalism, that we had overlooked the obvious: they had been bombarded with another kind of 'mind changing' drama and suspected that was what we wanted from them. Time pressures on a soap are crucial, so the bottom line was, they were being paid handsomely for their services and would have to trust to our good intentions.

Soaps are crafted things and soap writers in Britain have absorbed years of soap technique through watching and listening to the product. The Romanian writers had seen, only recently, North American and Latin American soaps in which character changes are achieved without regard for logic or verisimilitude. If someone can wake up in the shower and reveal that the last batch of episodes were but a dream, why can't a character be sniffing lilacs flowering in an urban garden in central Bucharest in December? We explained that the audience would be looking out of their windows on the same city and be seeing snow, dead stick bushes and trees.

The 'issues' the soap had a brief to tackle also created a problem. The western European consensus on racism, minority rights and dignity had not filtered through to Romania. Fighting prejudice in the population had to be suspended whilst we tackled it amongst the writers:

'No one from that part of Romania would ever have an illegitimate child.'

'All Jews are rich.'

'All Gypsies steal.'

'If a woman is divorced by her husband, it's always her fault.'

'You can spot a homosexual man from a long way away by the way they walk.'

'Lesbians just haven't met the right man.'

And on and on and on... All those years of Ceausescu's unpredictable loony rule, in a country almost hermetically sealed from outside influences, had had a deadly effect. We fought, we argued, we reasoned. We shall never know if we convinced them by our arguments or whether they were just giving in to the foreign bosses, but slowly a microcosmic world was created. The fictional square began to be populated with three dimensional characters, some comic some tragic. Eventually we were ready to broadcast.

We had some contemporary marketing aids: baseball caps and T-shirts with the Soap's logo on them; a fridge magnet which came complete with instructions 'Hold against fridge door, it will stick!' We went on air daily for fifteen minutes. I proudly wrote the prologue to the very first episode.

The press decided to ignore us. Radio Romania decided to ignore us. We worked in a vacuum of closed office doors. Was anybody out there listening?

Slowly, the letters began to trickle in from distant regions of the country. We received bags of mail thanking us for airing issues that had never been aired before:

'Thank you. I thought I was the only one with that problem'.

We hosted a symposium on modern drama techniques. The audience was composed of writing lecturers from the universities and their students. A solid barrage of contempt hit me. A distinguished professor announced:

'The ordinary people are too stupid to appreciate our work, so we don't write for them.'

The students nodded obediently.

'Drama is for the elite and the educated.'

The students nodded again.

And so on. One 'student' introduced himself to me and battered me with intrusive questions about my personal life. I was suspicious. My doubts were confirmed when, after I watched him to the exit, he reappeared an hour later, in the Director of Broadcasting's office. They both looked suitably sheepish when they saw me seeing them. Romanians always leave their office doors open except when you are looking for them.

We had held back on one storyline. Romanian prejudice against homosexuality was epic. Under Ceausescu convicted Gays were given a choice. Seven years in prison or inform on your friends for the secret police. Discussions had been held with representatives of Gay rights organisations. Despite the revolution, Gay people were still being evicted from their apartments, dismissed from their jobs; the seven year prison sentence was still in force. The subject was due for review in Parliament. I wanted to test the power of radio-drama. We decided to go ahead with the story.

I announced it at the script meeting. A strange reaction. Off colour jokes, embarrassment, and I was given several of, what my mother would call 'old fashioned looks'. To demonstrate my commitment to the story, I 'came out' to the crew.

The producer had taken me aside before the script meeting:

'I'll support you all the way with this story, but I think you should expect trouble.'

I knew what she meant. We already had proof that we were being spied on. It seemed inevitable that we had a spy in our midst. My paranoia during the discussions of this new storyline was reaching new heights, but I am stubborn and I decided this was too important to back down over. I had heard too many first hand accounts of the suffering of Romanian Gays.

Later in the meeting tempers flared. The writers had complete freedom, but I was insistent that the character should be introduced in the context of a story not connected with his sexuality. (We had pioneered this approach on *The Archers* with the introduction of the first Gay character, Sean Myerson.) Once the character was liked by the other characters and the audience, then and only then could his 'gayness' become an issue. After a gruelling day, the character was in place.

I was due to fly back to Britain the next day, so it was after a long farewell dinner that I returned to my hotel room. As I opened the door, I sensed something. Switching on the light revealed chaos. My suitcase contents were thrown everywhere. Drawers hung open. In the bathroom, an especially spiteful touch, the tops had been removed from the contents of my toilet bag, which had been upended into a gooey, sticky mess.

I didn't sleep much that night. I still had to get out of Romania – a lengthy and depressing business at the best of times. I was held back from the seemingly endless passport queue. I stood next to the door marked 'Security Police'. Eventually, just before my flight was called, I was called to the desk, stared at for about five minutes then cursorily waved through. At the door leading to the tarmac another queue. As I waited I was aware of being stared at by an airline official. As my time came he stared even harder at my lapel, where I wore a small BBC World Service badge. He leant close to me:

'BBC World Service?'

'Yes.'

'Thank you. You helped us keep our sanity.'

And he waved me through. If the power of radio-drama is still strong enough to disturb secret policemen; if it justifies the use of police informers and spies; if, in spite of censorship and repression, it succeeds in winning an affectionate place in the hearts of strangers in the former Soviet empire – then radio-drama won't be dying just yet.

THE PRODUCERS

DEVELOPING WRITERS FOR RADIO –
THE PRODUCER'S PERSPECTIVE
by Tanya Nash

What radio-drama means to me.

I think radio-drama is a magical medium to write for. The intimacy of the experience, as the play unfolds in the listener's mind, means you can make a very powerful and lasting impression on your audience. One reason for this is that the listeners conjure up their own pictures as they listen; pictures which might have additional personal references for them. Incidentally, this process can work is in reverse. Occasionally, when I've heard a play repeated, I can remember the task I was doing as I listened the first time. So there is no other experience like it.

Radio-drama is an extremely versatile medium to write for, requiring the combined imagination of film writer, playwright and novelist: film writer, because the best radio plays move between locations with the fluidity of film, whereas static ones are aurally dull; theatre playwright, because radio is also an artificial medium which requires a similar suspension of disbelief; novelist because a writer uses mostly words to conjure up pictures of the world and its characters, for the listener to realise it fully. Common to all three crafts are the creation of character and story.

What kind of dramas does BBC Radio want?

Whenever I meet a new writer they always ask me what am I looking for at the moment. Unlike television drama, which does look for specific genres at certain times, radio-drama is not so rigorously dominated in this way. So I always reply that I'm looking for the material that they feel compelled to write. I have found that the most interesting scripts come from a writer's passion. As writing is often an arduous task, why not work on what inspires you most.

The BBC's Radio 3 and Radio 4 are the major broadcasters of radio-drama. So I will concentrate on their demands. You can hear at least one new play every day of the week, which means that a lot of original material is required. The commissioners and listeners to these stations still appreciate the individual voice of a writer above formula and genre. BBC Radio does like to commission genre pieces such as detective stories. However, unlike television drama, it is not wedded to creating many long running series because the listeners prefer single dramas. I use the word 'voice' here to represent a writer's individual style and opinions. This means that there is plenty of scope for a wide variety of radio writers and subject matter.

BBC radio-drama does not exist in a social vacuum and it has paid attention to the idea of branding its product. Research has shown that listeners like to know the type of material they might expect to hear at a particular time of day. For example, radio adaptations of stage plays are broadcast on Sunday evenings on Radio 3 when they know listeners can give their full concentration to them. Or, late morning, on Radio 4, you can hear a variety of comedy series where the style may be familiar and the material more accessible because listeners will combine their listening with other tasks. For this reason, I advise all writers of radio-drama to listen regularly to the output and become familiar with the different types of plays and the times of day they are broadcast. You can then answer for yourself the question 'What are they looking for?' and focus your material accordingly. However, a word of warning. I am not recommending that you only create more of what you hear. Your originality is still important to hang on to. Instead, try and see where your ideas might belong in the schedules. Ultimately, it is the producer's job to decide this but it helps if you understand the process as well. I think, also, you should listen critically. If you are new to radio-drama make notes of what you think does and doesn't work, to help you gain an understanding of the medium. If you listen regularly, I hope that you will be pleasantly surprised at the wide range of material broadcast and the diversity of cultures and social backgrounds portrayed on these stations compared to other dramatic media.

Finding a producer.

How do I discover new talent and how do you find yourself a producer? As a producer, I keep a close eye on new writers working in the theatre and television and create links with a variety of writers' workshops, groups and courses. If I like a writer's work, then I will contact them and see if we can find ideas to work on. The BBC occasionally sets up competitions to search for talent in an area perceived as being under-represented. For example, *First Bite* was the third competition of its kind, run in 1995, to encourage new young writers under 30 to radio. More recently, in 1999, *Chasing the Rainbow* was a BBC Birmingham initiative to find more Afro-Caribbean and Asian writers from the Midlands. These schemes are run to say that the door is open to all new talent. As writers, I encourage you to write all the time and not just wait for a scheme to send in your work.

There are two main ways to find yourself a producer. First of all, you can send a script, unsolicited, to your nearest BBC drama department and then work with the producer who replies to you. Secondly, you can listen to the output and write a more personal letter to a producer whose work you genuinely admire and hope that they feel equally inspired by you. Please do this honestly and don't send the same script to every producer in the *Radio Times*. Each script sent to the BBC is logged on computer, so your efforts will be discovered and your attempt at the personal touch discredited. Occasionally, as the BBC's divided up into regions, you may find that your work is redirected to the department nearer to where you live. This has its advantages in cheaper travel costs and phone calls when discussing work with your producer.

As well as in-house producers, there are quite a few independent drama producers working for the BBC. They might also be worth contacting. Details can be found either via the Radio Academy or BBC Radio 4. The BBC has a list of preferred independent companies, so it is worth finding out who they are first of all. Sending your work to an independent company could possibly give you less chance of getting your work produced because the majority of radio-drama production is still produced in-house. However, I firmly believe that the best ideas get made whichever avenue you choose. Finding a producer is also about establishing a good, creative relationship.

The development process: your calling card is your script.

When an unsolicited script lands on my desk, I look for a strong story, told in an interesting and thought provoking way. What I don't want is a predictable tale told by stereotypical characters who speak in clichés. In my experience, the best playwrights combine sharp observation of the world around them with their own imagination to provide that original voice or vision. This applies to whatever they choose to write about from, autobiography to fantasy.

When you have an unusual story that your are burning to tell, it can be easier to get a producer interested in it. However, what do you do if your inspiration is popular subject matter? For example, the story could be a universal one about relationships, or you are fascinated by a well documented period of history. What gives the successful writer the edge over others is that they have something to say about the world they have created. However, beware of making your characters mouthpieces for dialectic. To make this theory work, you must make sure that opinions fit a character and their motivation. The other way not to do this is to have your main protagonists behave in a predictable and clichéd way, unaffected by any interpretation you have given to setting and minor characters; your voice should be well integrated with the whole piece. However, when a writer is aware of what their play is about and the themes within it, the world of the play is enriched. One final point about popular subject matter: there will be times when you may have to let an idea go because it has been done quite recently. Part of being a successful writer is having many stories to tell and not just one.

When you decide on what you want to say about your fictional world, you should also consider the contemporary relevance of your story for the audience. I believe it is important to distinguish the two thoughts. They are slightly different. If your opinions are out of date or uninformed by current thinking, then the audience and, more importantly the commissioners, will not be interested. However well written your play is, it will feel dated. Note that dramatic styles as well as opinions are affected in this way. Think of those early television police shows. Not only have the stories changed today, but the pace of storytelling and filming styles are radically different and are evolving all the time. Radio-drama is no different.

Let me clarify the point about contemporary relevance from the perspective of commissioners and producers. They should always ask you, 'Why should this story be told now?' None of us lives in total isolation and to differing degrees we absorb current social thinking from the media around us; radio, television, advertising, newspapers, and cinema all reflect back to us current trends. Satirical comedy is the most striking genre to examine this point because I think all good comedy has to be socially relevant. For example, in the 1980s Harry Enfield' s character *Loads A Money* was immensely popular because he typified a type of man created by Thatcher's Britain. Another interesting example is the huge success of the BBC radio and television comedy show *Goodness Gracious Me* in the late 1990s. I believe this happened because of changes in British society caused by the coming of age and prosperity of second generation British Asians. They now felt comfortable with their dual cultural identities and had something to say about living in multi-cultural Britain. So the comedy show reflected and commented on these current social changes via humour. We, the audience, appreciate the humour because we relate it to our experiences and the world around us.

This point about contemporary relevance is equally important when writing and re-examining historical plays. For example, can we understand the characters in a Greek drama without using Freudian psychology? It is possible but we have to make a conscious effort to do so. Most of your audience will not do this unless you make sure that this is the way you want them to understand it. Then you have to ask yourself, why would you want to do this? Even if you wanted to make a point about changes in social thinking, I still believe this can only be done in relation to contemporary beliefs. Remember, Shakespeare had no qualms about rewriting history to make social comment.

Development – the first stage.

If a writer is very inexperienced, then they must be prepared to write several complete drafts of their play, with a producer's guidance and for no payment, until the producer thinks it is of a high enough standard to win a commission. This work is vital for two reasons. The commissioners have so many plays to choose from that they don't need to take the risk on the potential of an undeveloped idea. They tend to select ones they can see are already good enough. Secondly, from the producer's point of view, this is necessary to establish whether or not the writer will be able to deliver a script to the required standard should a commission be won. Once writers are more experienced, then they can submit treatments to secure work. Writers who are experienced in other dramatic forms, such as theatre and television, can submit scripts from those media as samples of their writing. However, if you think a particular play would translate well to radio, then it is vital you send a treatment of how you would do this with your script. The producer will want to feel confident that you have a genuine interest in the medium, as well as gain an insight into your understanding of radio-drama.

Pitfalls to avoid when offering plays from other media for radio.

One mistake writers often fall into is thinking that if a stage play has a lot of dialogue then it will make good radio. This is not necessarily true. If the play seems clumsy and over-written on stage, then radio will only magnify this mistake. A further point to watch for when offering stage plays for radio is that they are often quite static, set entirely in one location. This can make for dull radio-drama, especially if the dialogue meanders along. Don't underestimate the magical experience for the listener, when conjuring up an exciting location from only sound. Remember my first point about the power of the listener's individual pictures. For example, the sound of surf and mention of country/location will transport the listener to the beach and possibly bring with it pictures of their own experiences on a tropical beach. With film, television and theatre scripts you also have to consider how important it is to actually see the action. Some visual situations can be portrayed through words, but at other times this can be clumsy, particularly in action drama. 'He's got a gun!' does sound rather awkward and can slow up the action. If a play works by visualising two sets of action simultaneously, or from the mistaken identity of twins, that can be hard to achieve on radio. Some comic writing relies on an actor's expressions for its laughs rather than the dialogue or visual comedy business which only a studio audience can see. Again, this won't work on radio. When you submit a treatment for adaptation, this is where you suggest how any problems might be solved. The producer will always be happy to offer advice and guidance if you have shown an understanding of the problems involved.

In many towns and communities there are writers' groups which meet regularly and where work is discussed and developed. These groups, often attached to theatres, are usually open to writers of all abilities and are a valuable way of developing talent. The BBC does not run writers groups in this way. However, at times, in the slightly random fashion of the open competitions mentioned earlier, it will target up-and-coming writers and nurture them for radio-drama. These writers will have already established a reputation for themselves in other media or from working for a while with a radio producer. For less experienced writers, I would recommend joining a local or national writers group as it is important to gain constructive critical exposure for your work from more than one source. You probably won't find one exclusive to radio-drama. Local theatres and libraries are a good first place to look, along with the *Writers' Guild* and the *Writers' and Artists' Year Book*. As well as helping with feedback on your work, they can also make you aware of any competitions and writing schemes coming up and be a source of support. Writing is a lonely business.

The production process.

Once an idea has been commissioned, the producer then adopts the role of script editor and gives detailed feedback on each draft. Compared with television and theatre, radio-drama production is rapid and this will usually occur over a few months with up to three drafts being developed. An inexperienced writer may need to write more. However, this is a one-to-one process with no other input from members of the BBC at the development stage. A good producer will help you find the way to say what you want to write rather than impose their interpretation on your material. For this reason, I remind you to know what your play is about and its themes. At times your ideas will not be clear, but if you know what inspired them, then the producer can help you portray your vision.

Every writer is invited to attend the recording of their radio play. It is a vital part of the development process for a script, whatever the experience of the writer. The read through is usually the first time when the script is given life off the page. The actors will have made some preparation for playing their characters, often with tips from the producer. However, it is the rehearsal of each scene which irons out any confusions or dud lines. The writer's role in this process is to clarify the meaning of any dialogue and character motivation for the actors. They should also be prepared to rewrite lines which don't work with the help and guidance of the producer and cast. Very occasionally, whole scenes may have to be rewritten in the rehearsal process. This is rare because the radio-drama production process is very rapid. For example, a 30-minute drama is rehearsed and recorded in a day and a 60-minute drama in two days. So, extensive rewrites should have been done at the script editing stage. A writer may also be called on to look for cuts if the script is too long after the read through, or write more scenes if the drama is too short. I believe that it is important for writers to see their work as a living being which isn't finished until the play is finally edited.

The editing of a recorded play is the one time when the writer isn't present. They now have to trust their work entirely to the producer and the studio editor. It is rare for any large changes to made at this stage. Usually, the only changes are cuts to the script to be make it fit the exact time allowed for each slot. I'm always surprised by how much can be cut from a script at this stage without any loss to the whole. Indeed, it is often enhanced.

When working with a new writer after their play has been produced, I think it is important to talk about what has been learnt to help with their next script.

The points made in this article are relevant to all writers, irrespective of their background. I believe all writers should have confidence in their ideas but also be open to advice and feedback. Good luck.

BRINGING THE STORY TO LIFE
Penny Leicester

I want you to accompany me through this article as though you were the producer and director of your own radio play. In radio, the producer and director are one; so I shall call you The Producer.

I grew up in the BBC. I have been through the bogs and boilers to the green rooms and heady heights of production with some of the great talents in the writing and acting world. I have been incredibly privileged. I joined the BBC as a studio manager; that meant I pressed the buttons on the disk and tape machines, and mixed and recorded the programmes across the output of the Domestic and World Service: news, sport, magazines, features, music and drama. (I particularly enjoyed slipping the mats in Radio 1.) I worked in the radio-drama script unit and produced single plays, poetry, readings and long-running drama serials. I also write, have children, and now freelance over the world as a Soap Consultant. (That's what it says on the business card; and I'm rather scared, and proud of it). I also work in the corporate and commercial world, from audio gallery guides to training and telephone chat lines. Everywhere I work, the experience and the programme sounds and formats I work in nourish the sound and develop the structure of my own writing.

Why am I showing you my CV? Because I want you to put aside your mice and pens and listen. You can't write for radio if you don't listen. Listen to the sounds out there; listen to the programmes. The most important single element in a radio-drama production is the script; but it is going to have to be especially good because of all the media, radio is the easiest to switch off or over, and radio mercilessly exposes the mediocre. To put it bluntly, you are going to have to use every storyteller and programme-maker trick there is to grab your listeners, to excite, entice, inform and entertain them. It's the sound you make as you tell your story that's going to count.

As a writer, you will have worked extensively on the text of your play; but have you worked on the sound? Have you heard every moment of every scene? Have you imagined how the listener will hear it? I asked this question at a workshop in Romania, and a young writer responded: 'I write for myself. That is what matters'. But in radio that is precisely what does not matter. The radio listener is on his/her own; the writer needs to actively involve that individual in the creative process of bringing the play to life. You, the writer, must connect with the listener and enable him or her, through sound, to create landscape, scenery, costumes, characters and action. (When you next buy a novel by Charles Dickens, I recommend you choose the edition without the illustrations of Phiz or Cruikshank. Marvellous though they are, they are not your illustrations.) TV dramatisations are very satisfactory and extremely comfortable; like a ready-made meal. But your involvement as the viewer remains passive. I believe that a good radio dramatisation is the only one in which the story will truly come to life; and that is because your imagination has been actively and creatively involved.

Now you may say: it is the job of the producer and the sound engineers to add the soundscapes to the words you provide in the text of the script; and they do. But to be a good radio writer I believe you should write as though you are the producer and the sound engineer. You should, as you write, use every element of sound at your disposal: the words, the FX (sound effects), music, and silence. And the greatest of these is silence.

Radio starts in silence. Imagine dawn. Go to the BBC sound FX library and you will find several disks labelled: 'Dawn'. Play them. The CD Dawn Chorus is a cacophony of birds, be they in woodland or urban environment. But now imagine dawn. Where does it start? In silence. To capture the first streak of light in the sky, you start in black. A faint murmur of wind is then perceptible to the ear. Then you may hear the first waking bird, mid-distance, as it starts its tentative song. A beat of silence, as you search the skies for light; then the bird is answered by another in the background. Leaves start to rustle. A bird in the foreground now starts to sing. And so on. The sound of dawn is sound across time in a landscape made up of the perspectives of the foreground, mid-distance and background. Time and perspective.

Your words may be telling the story of a woman dying in her farmhouse bedroom – as dawn breaks. Now you'll need to add a sound that enables the listener to see the 'farm at dawn' in the picture. (The milk cart and cockerel could do it. But you run the risk of creating a sound cliché which destroys the connection between you the writer and your listener.) You want a sound which in the imagination says: 'humans' and 'habitation'. One dog bark heard in mid-distance may be enough. (Each country has it own distinctive soundscape. I played a tape of a play without words to a group of producers from countries in Africa. What had been a clear sound story to the Radio 4 listener became a random sequence of sounds telling a different story to each different country. The dawn sound of October in Kigali, for example, would include the crash of a ripe avocado off the tree onto the tin roof – that, and the scattering of the local monkeys followed by the barking of a dog.)

Go back now to the dying woman in her room. The dog has informed us that people are somewhere in the landscape. Now you need to focus the scene: you need to take the listener from the outside to the inside of the room. How? Think like the cameraman. One option would be to track from the exterior picture into the room; not dissolving through the walls but entering, literally, through the window. Radio tracks such a shot by reducing the stereo ambient sound picture to a point of sound which can be placed as a fixed point. Here the background dawn sounds would be reduced to the point of sound heard from the window – left, right, or centre of the room. As you cross from the exterior into the room, the listener will also hear the acoustic change from exterior to interior room.

The camera now needs its focus. It could be close on the window, or it could be on the small fire in the grate, or it could be the sounds of the woman's laboured breathing. Now the door opens, the grieving husband enters and the scene begins. How much time have we taken with this soundscape? 15 seconds, if that. But in that 15 seconds we have turned the dark to light; we have prepared the listener for what is to come. We have stimulated their imagination and used their imagination to involve them in the drama.

FX EXT   (exterior) COUNTRYSIDE.
0545. DAWN.
SLIGHT WIND. BIRDS. IN DISTANCE, DOG BARKS.
CROSS TO INT: (Interior) FARM BEDROOM
THE WOMAN BREATHES WITH DIFFICULTY

DOOR OPENS.

Scripted words releasing so much information! Here is the draft stage direction for a scene from a Russian Soap Opera:

> *Vlad, with his bodyguards, waits in the old galvanising warehouse for the showdown with Gleb.*

This is the studio script of the same scene:

> *INT: GALVANISING WAREHOUSE. 1500. RAIN*
> *Dimu is leaning in the doorway, nervously watching the road. Edik, by the broken window, is biting his nails. Jacky is with Edik – peering out onto the rain-filled yard. Vlad is on microphone, casually smoking a cigarette.*

The difference between draft script and studio script is that the writer has filled in his scene with – to put it crudely – the 5 Ws of stage directions: Who is speaking? Where are they? What are they doing? Why are they doing it? And when?

The writer has rethought his scene and written it as though he were the producer and cameraman. He has set the focus: he has decided the listener should see the scene from Vlad's point of view. The camera is in close-up on Vlad. The other characters – his bodyguards – have now been placed in the scene and in the action. Now the scene can begin.

The radio writer should visualise and direct the focus and action. In a TV studio script, the directions for the camera outnumber the words of the dialogue. In radio, you need to incorporate the direction frame into the text. Not easy. If you have read Tom Stoppard's *The Real Inspector Hound*, you will know what I mean. Here is an example of a frame which has been incorporated unsuccessfully into the text.

INSPECTOR	Why... that's a body spread-eagled on the floor.
CONSTABLE	It's a woman's body.
INSPECTOR	She is not wearing any clothes.
CONSTABLE	How many times has she been shot?
INSPECTOR	I can see 3 bullet entry points.
CONSTABLE	She is a fine russet-haired woman.
INSPECTOR	Good lord; she must be the wife of the British Ambassador. He reported last week that his russet haired wife of 43 was missing.
Etc.	

Radio dialogue is not easy to write. It has to contain more information than a TV or filmscript; and it has to sound natural, even though it contains more information than everyday speech. The trick is slow-release. Just as the sound effects add information, so within your scenes you release information at the moment in time when it is necessary for the listener to see or hear what you want him/her to see. The listener doesn't need the full exposition in one go. Overload the first scenes and he or she will switch off or over, however good the content of your script. Your priority should be to engage your listener; then release information.

If radio dialogue is not easy, structure is; or should be, so long as you think radio rather than theatre. You don't need curtains; you don't need entrances and exits: like film, you get to the point, set the new dilemma or question, and then move on.

If TV has the rule that the dialogue should never make the camera redundant, then radio has the structural rule that the listener must never get lost. So long as the listener knows where he or she is and why, your structure is working. But are you exploiting the possibilities?

Think of the difference between the novel and the radio play. If a novel works by evolution, a radio script works by revolution. However linear or not the story of your radio script, however multi-layered the events, however many pieces there are in the stained-glassed window, the conclusion will bring the structure into a full circle.

For example; if there is an incident in a character's past which informs the action of the present, the simple radio structure will follow a linear path whereby the character today recalls the near present in the light of what happened to him in the past. Three time-levels. The character looks back on the past to explain the events that happened to him in the recent present. Once the explanation is there, the circle is complete. But there are more revolutionary possibilities available to the writer of a radio script. Take away, for example, one of the time elements. Don't look back. Now try to structure the play so that the character and action are in the present. Now break the past event into pieces, like the pieces of a jigsaw puzzle. In the action of the present, each time the character is forced into a situation of stress, a piece from the past can flash before him (flashback). As the play approaches its climax in the present, the pieces will nearly complete the picture of the past event. The listener has become gripped by the need to find out what is the puzzle that drives the character to act as he does in the present event of the story; what is the cataclysmic event which is about to happen caused by whatever it was that happened in the past? The listeners are involved by their responsibility to gather the pieces and fit them together. Only when the listener has all the pieces will the play make its circle.

The structure of the radio play has been given new freedoms by the increasing use of location recording and the opportunities provided by digital editing at the post production stage. More and more writers and producers think of radio as film; scenes are sequences. The tracking shot that was nearly impossible in the recording studio is now a simple affair with a hand held stereo microphone and a portable recorder. You can now run down the stairs, into the street, jump into the car and roar off. You can cut from the chase into the cellar where the hostage is held. You can split screen the action by the use of radio microphones. You are with the villain coming down the steps to the cellar. And you are hearing this from the hostage's point of view at the same time.

But as a writer for radio you should still be asking: how can I make the visual picture work with the right amount of information using up the minimum amount of precious transmission time? The action scenes which work in one way on television and film may work better on radio when viewed from another and different direction. For example:

> It is Sunday. Two youths are walking down the street. They spot a car with the key in the ignition. They jump in and off they go for the joy ride. One of the kids is more dominant than the other.

Visually there are many ways to do this. A man is washing his car, for example. He runs out of water. Goes into his house. The camera shows us the key in the ignition. In the car mirror, or in the reflection from the polished bonnet, we see two lads approaching. You can see the dominance of one of the lads by the way he grabs the jacket of the other and pushes him in to the car. And off they go for their joy ride.

Now try this for radio. You don't want to rely on information-driven dialogue of the kind: 'He's left his keys in the ignition. He's asking for it. Come on!' Nor do you want to lose your valuable transmission minutes creating an action sequence which might not be necessary to further the plot at this point. A radio alternative is to find a new direction, a different structural approach. You could start the sequence in the car as it roars off; and the dominant character crows while the other remains silent.

There are many ways of writing both the TV and radio version of the above scene. The decision for you is: At which point in the plot do you need to start and finish? And your next decision is: At which moment in the scene do you need to start and finish. Often, if you look at your script, you will find that you can start a third of the way into your scene, and cut out of it once your point has been made. Radio tells its stories within a very concise structure. You could cut the opening third: 'Hello come in. Sit down. Would you like a cup of tea'. And cut out of the scene at the point where the dilemma has been set: 'Oh no. What should we do now?'

Let's go back to the soundscape of the dying woman script. You have thought about the camera angles: how you want the listener to see the scene. Now it's time to consider what effect you want your sounds to have. Dawn is a pretty sound. It contrasts with the sadness of the scene in the room. As a writer, you have 'Thomas Hardy' and 'Emily Brontë' options: nature is either impassive or it reflects the emotional state of the characters at that point in their story (pathetic fallacy). Sound can complement or contrast. It sets mood as well as landscape. And, of course, it provides information: dawn.

Sound can also prepare:

Preparation: The man walking back from the pub who is about to beat up his wife is talking happily to his mate about the football match tomorrow. As they walk, in the distance you have scripted that we hear the sounds of a drunk crashing into a bin, or knocking the milk-bottles.

Preparation: In Scene 1, the man who kills his wife by the end of the play is taking a can of lager from the fridge as he tells his wife he won't be eating the dinner she has prepared because he is going out with his mates. She quietly puts the dinner to one side and makes no complaint. In this scene, you will have scripted the moment at which he pulls that ring on the can of lager. Think of the sound it makes. It is an aggressive punctuation. Place this sound at the right moment in the scene within the dialogue and it will provide the information hidden beneath the apparent calm on the surface: intimations of the violence to come.

Literal sounds in radio plays work well as symbols. In the novel *Of Mice and Men*, John Steinbeck – with the consummate art of the film-maker – 'scripts' the literal sounds as symbolic motifs: every time something is about to happen which will change the course of events in the life of Lenny – the simple minded itinerant farm-worker – a bird takes off in flight. There is the flapping of wings as he bursts through the brush, and the sound of the pigeon that flies into the barn after Lenny has killed the wife of the boss's son. Steinbeck scores his books with a soundscape in the same way that you, the writer of a radio play, should do. The tip is to remember that you are trying to stimulate the imagination. Once you begin to overdo it, you will achieve the opposite effect. To create 'dawn' you decided to reject the noise on the FX CD Dawn. Less is more. (The sound of one hungry child crying is famine.) If you use sound merely to illustrate, you are in danger of entering the switch-off zone. You are disengaging your listener. For example:

> The soldiers marched down the street.
> *FX FEET MARCHING.*
> The buglers played.
> *FX BUGLERS.*
> The children laughed and sang.
> *FX CHILDREN LAUGHING AND SINGING.*

Once you make your listeners redundant, they will switch off or over.

Silence is a very precious sound in your radio play. At its most basic level, it is structural: it can mark the 'in' and 'out' of your scene sequences. It should also provide a rhythm to the structure: a scene that cuts to a beat of silence sets a different pace to a scene which fades the sounds to black. Why am I telling you the obvious? Because if you haven't thought through the way your scenes connect, you haven't heard your play and if you haven't heard it, the listener certainly won't. Silence sets the beat.

'Pauses' or 'beats' are the 'looks' that work on camera between the characters in the play. It is not what has been said, but what is left unsaid; the silence marks the icebergs lurking beneath the surface. Silence marks the moment when the characters connect. It also gives a radio listener the moment to see the action, and make the connection. In *Of Mice and Men*, Lenny breaks the neck of the wife of the boss's son. He leaves the barn to hide in the brush by the river. The moment of silence comes as he makes his exit from the barn. Steinbeck keeps us in the barn. Silence descends. We know the body lies in the straw. The moment is held. Nothing happens. We are given space to make the connection – the man is lost. The silence is broken when a pigeon flies in and circles before finding its way out again. Steinbeck has written this moment into his narrative; the playwright will write this into the action, FX and dialogue of the scene.

As a script editor I fear the five capital letters, 'MUSIC' when they appear plonked at random into a script. Music is not a separate element but, like silence, it is organic to every element of the play; and it will have existed in your very first intimations of the idea. Music can provide information, period and place. It can create the mood, and it can underscore the action or emotions. It can work by contrast to the action and emotions. It creates a style. It makes the connections. It sets the rhythm. And it attracts, delights and engages the listener.

I started this article by saying that you, as the writer of a radio play, should think of yourself as the producer; but I see now that I have added considerably to your involvement in the success of your play. You are also the sound designer, cameraman, and musician. (With experience in the studio, when you see your play being recorded and edited, you will also write your scripts aware of the possibilities provided by the technology of digital editing in post-production.)

What I love about radio are its infinite possibilities. Nothing is impossible: a lump of rock can philosophise on the ages of man; a child can speak to its mother from the womb; the writer can take the listener to the Battle of Waterloo or to the spaceship Mir without bankrupting the budgets. But, to me, radio's greatest strength is its ability to creep up on a listener and shake him or her to the core. In a time when we have become anaesthetised by television images of violence, war, deprivation, displacement and famine; in a time where celebrities front campaigns in order to shake us out of compassion fatigue, radio is, I believe, the most influential and powerful of all the media in that it speaks directly to the individual. It can break down barriers by raising awareness and promoting tolerance and understanding. (In the wrong hands, it can be used to devastating effect.)

That's a big responsibility for any writer of contemporary radio-drama. And you need all the help you can get. So listen. Listen to the sounds around you in the real world. Find the people who are the stories. Don't write from the isolation of your tower, but always connect to the listener. Listen to what he or she is listening to; listen to the output. One last tip, or trick to keep up your sleeve: always be different. Just when the listener thinks he's got you sussed, pull another rabbit from the hat.

THE HEART AND SOUL OF THE WRITER
David Ian Neville

What kind of writers write for 'soaps' or long-running serials? Are they hacks? Are they journeymen? Do they just write the dialogue and follow given storylines religiously?

Although this chapter is about writing for radio soaps, any knowledge you have of TV soaps will be useful.

A cursory glance at the credits over the years for *Eastenders, Coronation Street, Brookside, The Archers* and many other soaps will reveal the names of many well known theatre, television and film writers. It's not simply the case that many of them learnt their craft and made their name in the industry writing for such programmes; the experience of soap is much more complex. I'm sure that each writer would tell a different story of their experiences and of what – if anything – it added to their skills or resources as a writer.

The quantity of material required by soaps means that it is one section of the media business that offers a great deal of work to writers of drama. Writing to a tight brief or storyline, using established characters and relationships, can either be restricting or challenging. The challenge is to play with the component parts that you are given, invest whatever it is you've got as writer in it, and come up with scintillating scripts that stand up as good television or radio-drama. The added bonus, apart from being paid for all this, is that more people will watch or listen to your episode or episodes than will ever see one of your original plays in a theatre – well, unless it runs for years and years in the West End. Check out the TV and radio ratings for details of audiences sizes, but just for example, approximately one million people listen to each episode of *The Archers* and over 80,000 people listened to each episode of *Station Road* – the daily drama serial that ran on BBC Wales for two years. And think how many people watch the TV soaps. Even on a bad night – millions! But as they say, size isn't everything. Audience appreciation or stimulation is also important. So if people are talking about what has just happened or might happen in their favourite soap, things are going well!

Soaps are part of our culture. When they are good and the stories are relevant or exceptionally well crafted, or extremely controversial, they can set the agenda for discussion in pubs, playgrounds, work, home, the media and even the Houses of Parliament. Soaps have the potential to be trivial and banal, but also to be powerful stages for exploring dramatic issues and situations that can affect our lives.

If Shakespeare and Dickens were alive today, would they be writing for one of the soaps? Dickens wrote many of his great works in episodic form for magazines. Like other nineteenth-century novelists, he made part of his living by writing to demand. As Dickens's stories gripped the nation, more instalments were commissioned; and it's not hard to imagine that some twists and turns in the dramatic journey were invented to help boost circulation figures. Shakespeare re-worked existing stories and events from history to carve his dramatic works. Both Shakespeare and Dickens indulged in analysing and testing the human spirit, creating heroes and villains, and setting moral dilemmas for the public to debate. So, not that far from the job of writing for a long-running serial?

Some may feel that comparing the works of great writers to soaps is nothing short of criminal. There are good and bad plays and there are good and bad soaps. While soaps are by nature long-running, they are not by any means immortal. There is therefore a huge pressure on the producers to maintain the quality of the programme and retain the audience. There is also an ongoing pressure to invite new listeners or viewers into the habit of following the programme.

Although there are similarities in the way many long running serials are produced, they all operate their own unique system or routine. Each programme has its own set of guidelines, policies and stylistic idiosyncrasies. And if you want to write for a serial, you need to get to know the ropes fairly quickly.

I have worked on five different soaps as a writer and a producer. I don't, however, pigeon hole myself as a soap writer or producer. Working on these serials is only part of my creative work and only part of my life. Each in their own way has given me valuable experience and a creative opportunity to either write or produce for a large audience.

One thing I have learnt is that it is not just the viewer or listener that can become addicted to soaps. The production team and the writers can become addicted to the fictional world of the soap. But that is not a bad thing – if you are going to write for a programme, you need to know it inside and out.

The show, the system and the deadlines.

At the time of writing, there are two long running serials or soaps on British radio, *Westway*, the World Service's twice weekly serial; and *The Archers* on Radio 4. There is also a new serial being planned for the BBC Asian Network. Until recently there was also *Station Road*, the popular daily drama serial on BBC Wales. There are of course more soaps on television, from the home produced favourites such as *Coronation Street*, *Emmerdale*, *Family Affairs* and *Hollyoaks* to the Australian imports such as *Neighbours*, and *Home and Away*.

Using the word *soap* is contentious. It pigeon-holes and groups programmes that very often differ in subject, form, location, style and quality and have very little in common. Those who look down on *soaps* fall into a variety of categories. There are the people who never watch or listen to them so don't really know what's in them but think they do. There are those who instinctively feel that *soaps* dumb down and would prefer that everyone was only exposed to what they consider to be classic works. There are also some who think *soaps* are rubbish and a complete waste of time, but can't stop watching or listening to them!

If you want to write for a *soap*, you've got to like them – or at least like the one you want to work on. You've got to be able to enter into the world of the soap and play the game. What is the game you ask? More about the game later.

Soaps work on many levels. The storytelling can work on a simplistic basis or in a very complex form. Usually in a soap there are several stories being told at the same time. The programme is an ongoing tapestry of storytelling, with beginnings, middles and endings seemingly colliding at random. In practice, the positioning and unfolding of stories and their subsequent intertwining and interaction should be carefully planned for maximum effect.

The time-span of stories inevitably varies and for the writer it is important to be aware and understand how the unfolding of a story over weeks, months and even years can add to the storytelling. To write for a soap, you need to be a craftsman or woman and you have to enjoy your craft. You need to be a team player and yet you need to be independent.

Team player or solo star?

On serials like *Station Road* and *The Archers* a team or pool of writers contribute to the serial. While the writers don't write their scripts together, they do contribute to the devising and development of the stories. The writers attend monthly script meetings and ideas are discussed, debated and fleshed out for the next four weeks of the programme. A final storyline document is produced, and the writers work to this to create their week of scripts. Four writers from the team would be scripting at any one time, each writer working on their own week of scripts – five 15-minute scripts for *Station Road* and six 13-minute scripts for *The Archers*.

Before actually writing the scripts, each writer must produce a scene-by-scene breakdown of their week. The breakdown needs to give a comprehensive account of what will happen in each scene and list which characters are being used. The scene breakdowns are then edited by the programme's producers and feedback is given to the writers before they get the go-ahead to continue with the scripts.

On *Station Road,* writers got four days to devise and write their scene breakdown and ten days to write their scripts. Following delivery of scripts, there is a further three days for re-writes to be delivered. The deadlines are crucial to the smooth running of the programme and they have to be met by all who work on this type of drama be it for radio or television.

Writing as part of a team and to a storyline and tight deadlines will not suit everyone. Is it possible to be creative and retain your individuality as a writer within such systems? I believe that the quality and diversity of long-running serials depends on writers retaining their individuality and maintaining their creativity to the highest level. But if they have to stay shackled to the storylines, how is this possible? The writer has the freedom to choose how they tell the stories. They can decide what scenes to dramatise and which characters to focus on. There will always be discussion between the producers and the writers about the use of characters and choice of scenes. Inevitably there will be trade-offs and changes, times when one party will win or lose a particular debate. But in the main, after the storyline is produced, it is up to the writers to structure and cast their week.

The writer can find their own area of focus or particular angle in telling the stories. They must of course relate to the story on some level and in doing so they then find what they want to write about. The story is a vehicle for exploring people, issues, problems and situations. Through the use of given plots and characters, the writer can express their own voice in tone, mood and attitude.

The quality of the writing and script editing should ensure that the change of one writer's voice to another from week to week doesn't jar. The focus and emphasis may change, but the characters should still speak with the same voice and behave with a logic that belongs to their persona.

Structure, plot and formula.

The long-running serial or soap is one of the most dynamic evolutions of the ancient art of storytelling. The underlying aim of such programmes is to build and hold a loyal following of listeners or viewers. Like the storyteller in the marketplace, people can join at any time and hopefully understand and enjoy the ongoing story.

There are therefore conventions and rules that apply to such a genre. Each programme will of course set and adhere to its own set of rules. Some rules are absolutes, and some are open to considered interpretation.

For example, in *The Archers*, the main action is tightly focussed on the fictional village of Ambridge. There are forays beyond the boundaries of Ambridge to the nearby town of Borchester and occasionally further afield; but essentially the programme is about the people who live and work in and around Ambridge. In *Station Road*, the programme focused on the people who live in one particular part of the fictional Welsh valley town, Bryncoed. There were forays further afield to Cardiff, West Wales and beyond. But again the main action and interest was tightly focused in one particular community. If you like, the camera or microscope is focused tightly to give a close-up of a particular area rather than a wide shot or view of a large area.

The same approach is taken with characters, and in the main the concentration is on a regular set of characters rather than an ever-changing group.

So, if you think of soap as a game, the writers, the producers and of course the audience become very well acquainted with the component parts and the 'rules'. They know and come to expect that the characters can and will be pitted against each other in a variety of situations. Problems and emotional ammunition and injury are loaded onto the backs of certain characters and then the game begins. How will each character react? How will the actions of one character affect another character or a group of characters? Will the characters react in a predictable manner? Or will some new element in the story and situation lead them to act in a way which the audience doesn't quite expect but nevertheless will believe?

The game of soap can be endless. In simple terms, the writers devise a story and drip feed it to the audience. Throughout the telling of the story, the audience try to predict what will happen next. And no matter what happens next, if the story is good enough, the audience can discuss and disseminate it endlessly with friends and family.

There is another quite special dynamic to soaps or long-running serials. The very fact that that they are long-running means that the audience can get to know some of the characters over many years. This long-term relationship with a fictional character often means that members of the audience have a great affinity with that character – they may even have grown up with the character. So they know the character inside out – they've been there at all the big moments in that character's life. Perhaps the birth of their first child coincided with a fictional birth in their favourite soap; or they may have married at the same time as one of the characters. Shared memories include both real life events and fictional events.

I directed the episode of *The Archers* in which John Archer got killed in a farming accident. To this day, I still meet people who remember where they were when they heard that episode. The day after the episode was transmitted, almost every national newspaper carried an article about the character and the storyline. Many listeners had 'known' John Archer all his life. They were listening years back when he was born, they followed the trials and tribulations of his young life, and finally they 'mourned' his untimely death at the age of 21.

Soaps are constantly creating classic moments of contemporary drama. Some are only remembered in vivid detail by passionate fans, but other moments are witnessed and remembered by a much wider audience and thus enter the folklore of soap.

So what are the defining qualities of a soap writer?

The first is that the writer is able to operate as an individual and as part of a team. The script meetings can be fun and stimulating, but writing the scripts on your own to very tight deadlines can be a lonely job. In addition to this:

• The writer must enjoy working with and getting to know characters they haven't created. You will, if you're lucky, create significant moments in that character's life.

• You have to be generous with your creativity and enjoy feeding your thoughts and ideas into the collective melting pot.

• You have to be able to take on board ideas that you might not have originally agreed with but which have been 'bought' by the producers. Next, you need to find a way of making these ideas work both for you and the programme. Your doubts about a certain idea may be the key to finding ways of making the story stronger.

• You have to be good at finding your own way of telling a story, finding your angle and your focus.

• Finally you have to enjoy the fun of storytelling!

NOTES ON CONTRIBUTORS

Louise Page is a playwright, novelist and journalist. She was awarded the George Devine Award for her play *Salonika* in 1982 and was Resident Writer at the Royal Court Theatre 1982-3. She was a member of the *The Archers* writing team for ten years. Her work appears regularly on television, radio and in the theatre to critical acclaim. Many of her plays are published by Methuen.

Mick Martin is a former freelance playwright, theatre critic and teacher. He was a member of *The Archers* writing team from 1992 to 1998, and is the author of a number of plays for the stage and for radio. He has taught in universities in the UK, France and New Zealand. His arts journalism includes numerous reviews and features for *The Guardian* and various other national publications. He and his wife June now run an art gallery and picture-framing business in Salisbury.

Nick McCarty is a writer working across many genres. His work for radio includes numerous original plays and adaptations, including *A Tale of Two Cities*, which won a Sony Award for Best Adaptation. Work for television includes *Dangerfield, Casualty* and *Bergerac*. Nick has also written original plays for the theatre and written books for children and adults. He is currently working adaptation of *The Anonymous Venetian* by Donna Leon and on *The Nun and the Chasseur*, a play based on the love letters of a sixteenth century Portuguese Nun.

Mark Brisenden is a freelance comedy writer whose work has appeared on hundreds of BBC Radio comedy shows. having been performed by, amongst others, Spike Milligan, Roy Hudd, Alistair McGowan, Ronni Ancona, Dick Vosburgh, The Strange Dr Weird and The Marx Brothers (well, sort of). A former recipient of the prestigious BBC Light Entertainment Contract Writers Award he remains a passionate devotee of Old Time Radio. Hi-yo, Silver! Awaaaay!

Sue Teddern, a former window dresser and journalist, has written ten single plays for radio, including *Lonely This Christmas, From Galway to*

Graceland and *Picking Up the Pieces*. She created and wrote the six-part comedy-drama *Lucky Heather* and two series of *The Charm Factory*. Television work includes 13 episodes of *Birds of a Feather* (BBC1) and her own comedy-drama *Happy Together* (ITV1). Currently she has several sitcom and comedy-drama projects in development and has also worked as a script editor on *Manchild* (BBC2) and *Sir Gadabout* (ITV1). Sue is a regular tutor for The Arvon Foundation.

Christopher Hawes has taught and devised courses in many universities in this country and abroad. He has written journalism for the BBCi website and his book about being writer-in-residence at Kirklevington Grange is published by Waterside.

Debbie Barham died tragically in Easter 2003 aged just 26. Born of ex-Cambridge University parents, the 'Unsung Queen of Comedy', as she was once called, left school at the age of 15 with top exam grades to pursue her dream of being a comedy writer in London. She achieved that goal in the first year, becoming a commissioned writer for the BBC, went on to win a writers' competition in 1992, and became a contract writer for the BBC in 1994/5. She wrote prolifically for radio, and was a regular contributor to shows such as *The News Huddlines, Weekending, Loose Ends* and *The News Quiz*. Other radio work included a Radio 4 panto, a Radio 2 sitcom *The Elephant Man,* and *Cross Questioned* (a panel game devised by Debbie), and various other series for Radio 4 and Radio 5 Live.

She was equally prolific as a writer for TV, working for Bob Monkhouse, Clive Anderson, Rory Bremner, Graham Norton, Russ Abbott, Spitting Image, Lily Savage and Mel and Sue. She scripted the Olivier Awards in 2002/3, *Celebrity Driving School* in 2003, and a range of documentaries, fashion and chat shows.

Somehow she also found time to be a journalist (usually with the inevitable comedy treatment) and was a regular contributor to many national newspapers, *Punch* and *Private Eye*, computer and 'gadget' magazines, womens' magazines, sports columns, and wrote four books of her own.

Sam Boardman-Jacobs began writing single plays, documentaries and features for BBC radio drama with the legendary producer Piers Plowright and then going on to script over 500 episodes of Radio 4's *The Archers*. His training consultancy and dramaturgical work includes the BBC Black Broadcast, residential writing courses for the Arvon Foundation and Tŷ Newydd in North Wales as well as training Romanian writers in Bucharest to produce their first ever home-grown radio soap. He is currently Reader in Theatre and Media Drama at the University of Glamorgan where he jointly runs the MA in Scriptwriting.

Tanya Nash is a Bi-media producer for BBC Northern Ireland, working with writers to develop ideas for radio and television drama. Her work in radio-drama involves producing plays for Radio 3 and Radio 4 – acting as script editor, casting agent, director, and producer on commissioned plays.

Penny Leicester is currently working as an advisor to assist with the development of the new soap for the BBC Asian Network. She is still working on projects with writers abroad with the BBC World Service Trust. Her most recent piece of writing is the dramatisation for *Woman's Hour* of the novel by E.M. Forster *Where Angels Fear to Tread*.

David Ian Neville works as a Drama Producer, developing and producing plays and series for BBC Radio 4 and BBC Radio 3. Prior to joining BBC Scotland he worked for BBC Wales where he produced and helped set up the drama serial, *Station Road*. During the previous three and a half years he was a producer on *The Archers*, devising, storylining and directing a wide variety of stories. Before joining the BBC, he worked freelance as a writer, director and producer. Writing credits include: *Inside* BBC Radio 4; storylines for Lynda La Plante's TV series, *The Governor*; the award winning TV plays, *Martha & The Audition* for STV; *Across the Barricades* for Tag Theatre Co., and The New Victoria Theatre, Stoke-on-Trent; and the Fringe First Award winning play *Exile* produced at the Edinburgh Festival and The Bush Theatre, London.